PENGUIN T

THE BEST V

Sybille Bedford was born in Charlottenburg, Germany, and was privately educated in Italy, England and France. She published her first book, *A Visit to Don Otavio: A Traveller's Tale from Mexico* (first published under the title of *The Sudden View*), in 1953. Three years later she published her highly praised first novel, *A Legacy*. *The Best We Can Do* started her on a new direction and she covered nearly a hundred law cases in England, France, Germany and Switzerland in search of material for her book *The Faces of Justice*. She has recently published *Jigsaw: An Unsentimental Education: A Biographical Novel* (1989), which is forthcoming in Penguin. Sybille Bedford has contributed literary criticism and articles on travel, food and the law to numerous publications, including the *Spectator*, *TLS*, *Observer*, *Harpers & Queen*, *Vogue*, *New York Review of Books*, *The New York Times* and *Esquire*.

Sybille Bedford is a Fellow of the Royal Society of Literature and Vice President of PEN. She was awarded the OBE in 1981. She has been based mainly in France, England, the United States and Italy and now lives in London, where she is working on a new novel.

SYBILLE BEDFORD

THE BEST WE CAN DO

PENGUIN BOOKS

TO
EDA LORD

PENGUIN BOOKS

Published by the Penguin Group
27 Wrights Lane, London W8 5TZ, England
Viking Penguin Inc., 40 West 23rd Street, New York, New York 10010, USA
Penguin Books Australia Ltd, Ringwood, Victoria, Australia
Penguin Books Canada Ltd, 2801 John Street, Markham, Ontario, Canada L3R 1B4
Penguin Books (NZ) Ltd, 182–190 Wairau Road, Auckland 10, New Zealand

Penguin Books Ltd, Registered Offices: Harmondsworth, Middlesex, England

First published by Collins 1958
Published in Penguin Books 1961
Reissued with a new introduction 1989
1 3 5 7 9 10 8 6 4 2

Made and printed in Great Britain by
Cox and Wyman Ltd, Reading, Berks.

INTRODUCTION

The prosecution of Dr John Bodkin Adams for murder at the Old Bailey in London in March 1957 will go down in history as one of the great English criminal trials. Other doctors have been tried for murder, but not since Dr William Palmer of Rugeley was convicted at the same court almost a hundred years before had it been alleged that a medical man used his professional skill in order to kill a patient. Adams's trial lasted for three and a half weeks – that is seventeen days in court – and was to date the longest murder trial held in England.

In 1956 – the year of his indictment – Dr Adams was fifty-eight, and had been in private general practice at Eastbourne for over thirty-five years. The practice was large and lucrative, many of his patients being rich, old and female. He was a zealous nonconformist churchwarden; his hobbies were motoring and clay-pigeon shooting. He was unmarried and lived alone in a large Victorian house, looked after by a devoted elderly housekeeper.

During the summer of 1956 Eastbourne buzzed with rumours about Dr Adams and a number of 'mysterious deaths'. In September Scotland Yard sent senior detectives to investigate. Stories began to appear in the Press and were soon taken up by the (unfettered) international Press, who freely described Dr Adams as a latter-day English Bluebeard. In December the Doctor was arrested for the murder of a Mrs Morell. The preliminary hearing before the Eastbourne Magistrates' Court in January 1957 lasted a fortnight, and was conducted in public in spite of an objection by the defence. The prosecution alleged that the Doctor had also murdered two other rich patients for gain. These allegations of triple murder by a well-known local figure were publicized to all; very few people could have remained ignorant of the Press view of the Doctor's guilt.

Dr Adams was committed for trial in London instead of at the

Lewes Assizes in Sussex because of possible local prejudice. The exhumation of the bodies of two other patients of Dr Adams, on the day after he was charged with murder, hugely served to increase curiosity and prejudice. Nothing was ever heard of the result of these investigations, so it is fair to assume that they disclosed nothing incriminating.

Dr Adams was held in custody in Brixton Prison from December 19th 1956 until April 18th 1957; the actual trial began on March 18th. The Judge was Mr Justice Patrick Devlin (now Lord Devlin of West Wick). The Attorney-General, Sir Reginald Manningham-Buller (later Viscount Dilhorne), Q.C., M.P., with Malcolm Morris appeared for the Crown; Geoffrey Lawrence, Q.C., Edward Clarke and John Heritage were counsel for the defence.

It should be borne in mind that at the time capital punishment had not been abolished. Therefore the death penalty was still mandatory for a conviction of murder.

My intention in writing this book about the trial was to give an accurate and complete, if compressed, account of what happened in court – minute by minute, hour by hour, throughout those wearisome, taxing days: what was heard (and how this was said and received: the tone, the tempo, the inflections); what could be seen; what appeared to be collectively felt. I had never been satisfied with newspaper reporting of criminal trials – the truncation, the hourly chase after sensations, the inevitable fragmentation. There are, of course, good books about *causes célèbres*, though there too one usually finds a tendency to highlight drama instead of letting the impact of the recounted event strike by its own momentum; such books go in for the 'whole story', the background, the aftermath. I, for once, wanted to record solely from the point of view of an alert spectator for whom such truths as can be caught unfold *in* court – where the outcome is decided – and nowhere else. I set myself up, as it were, as a private member of the jury. Like a member of the jury, I tried to exclude previous knowledge from my mind: the rumours, the gossip, the Press reports of the preliminary proceedings before the magistrates at Eastbourne (which were quite different from what emerged in the Old Bailey at the actual trial). This is not as improbable a feat as it may sound; there is something about the ritual, the rigour, the gravity of an English High Court that is chastening and compelling.

Unlike a member of the jury, I was not forbidden to talk about the case in the corridors and pubs with my colleagues, who were foreign correspondents of the international Press (present in droves). Most of us had no access to the national Press, the died-in-the-wool crime reporters, who would have no truck with us outsiders. They sat in their well-placed press-box, and were tolerated as they scrambled in and out during proceedings to pass on a scoop or meet the next deadline.

I sat throughout on one or other of the benches beside the dock, a position which, if far from ideal, is worlds apart from the isolated heights of the public gallery – a place so remote that the men and women who have come to see justice done (if *that* was their wish) are reduced, after long hours of queueing, to peering at what is going on below as though through the wrong end of a telescope. (As a matter of fact, I had to queue for Day One, my journalist's credentials not having come through in time; I spent an entire night from 10 p.m. to 10 a.m., an interesting and exhausting experience I should not like to share again.)

One of the serious flaws of admission by queueing is that the member of the public cannot leave his or her hard-won seat during the luncheon or any other break without losing it – if they leave they have to queue in the street again from scratch. This means, if the trial is regarded as at all sensational, they will almost certainly not get in again before next morning and thus miss the afternoon session, and with it a sense of sequence, coherence, responsible participation. What keeps them going, one assumes, is the hope of hitting on a self-contained patch of drama.

What were my motives or qualifications? Much interest in, and a little knowledge of, the workings of the law; a belief in justice and the imperative necessity of justice in a civilized and humane society; my *métier* as a writer, a novelist – here in the role of observer rather than inventor; a great curiosity about human beings and their points of crisis.

Whenever the name of Dr John Bodkin Adams comes up, I am asked, 'Did he *do* it?' 'Was he *guilty*?' And I always answer, 'NO'.

As far as one can ever be certain of anything, the Doctor was no murderer.

A man charged with a great crime, with whatever aloofness the law may hold him innocent before the verdict, is nearly always presumed to have been not quite that after his acquittal. In the Doctor's case, the world to a spectacular degree did not presume him innocent *before* his trial. Doubt, reasonable and unreasonable, subsequently hung about him to the end of his days and after. During the trial almost everyone, in the street, at dinner-tables, in the Press, was animated by the casual conviction that the Doctor had open-handedly poisoned scores of elderly patients for the sake of legacies. Among the exceptions were the *Daily Express*; the trial Judge, Justice Devlin; and, if I may say so, after the bafflingly weak opening for the prosecution, myself. However, the really firm believers in the Doctor's innocence were those who knew him, his friends and, above all, his patients who were as fond of him as he was of them. I have come across a number of them over the years and their children and grandchildren – 'Oh, Dr Adams brought me into the world.' 'A kindly doctor,' they will say, '*comforting*, never late for a visit . . . Perhaps not a very up-to-date doctor . . .'

So what went wrong? Why were the ghastly tales of mass-murder and immoral gain allowed to spread? Why were they taken up by the police? There is an enlightening, and most entertaining, account of the antecedents and consequences of the case in Lord Devlin's lucid and unusual book (a trial Judge commenting on his own trial), *Easing the Passing*, written after the Doctor's death in 1983. Also, one may add, after the death of the Attorney-General, Sir Reginald Manningham-Buller – Mannerless-Bully as Bernard Levin used to style him in print in the *Spectator*; Lord Devlin calls him Reggie, and does not spare him any the less. Rightly so, I am inclined to say: the Adams prosecution, as it appeared to me, was botched and bungled and dull.

Well, how did it all start? It was a fact that a good number of the Doctor's patients died, as well they might considering that they were generally quite ill as well as old when they came to spend their declining years at Eastbourne. The point that provoked suspicion was that many of them left him cash legacies. The police reckoned the bequests to be as high as £3,000 a year over a decade or more (a tidy sum in the 1940s and 50s). The Doctor candidly told them that the legacies were in lieu of fees – he had a flourishing practice, a large income subject to surtax. So he told his patients not to pay him there and then, but to leave to him in their wills what they thought they owed.

You may think he was fiddling the Inland Revenue. You may think that it is perhaps not the most reassuring thing to be told by one's doctor (called in, say, for bronchitis), 'I'd rather you pay me in your will.' You may think that the Doctor was a rogue, a greedy rogue, but as Justice Devlin said in his summing-up, ' . . . a rogue and a murderer are miles apart.'

John Bodkin Adams was born in Northern Ireland in 1899. Both his father and his only brother died of influenza during or soon after the 1914–18 War. His widowed mother was a devout temperance campaigner (the boy was made to sign the pledge at the age of eight or nine). She is said to have broken up his engagement to a girl he wished to marry; he continued to live with his mother until her death in advanced old age.

It is significant that the Doctor qualified in Belfast in 1921, when morphia was still available over the counter. (During the war people used to send a tube of morphia tablets with the chocolate and warm socks to their loved ones in the trenches.) Thirty years on, the Doctor, an easy-going, somewhat lazy man (he seldom bothered to keep medical records), was still in the habit of prescribing quantities of morphia and heroin with a prodigal hand. The prosecution called the doses enormous. Whether all drugs prescribed were actually administered to the victim of the case, Mrs Morell (hers was the only death for which this pilloried 'mass-murderer' was ever tried), we shall never know. The nurses' records do not really say. Perhaps some of the drugs disappeared. There must have been carelessness, possibly dishonesty . . .

The great, the insuperable, weakness of the case against the Doctor was the absurd triviality of the alleged motive. Mrs Morell did not leave him, and never intended to leave him, a cash legacy. What she left to this most comfortably-off medical man was a chest with some silver. It was valued for probate at £275 (Mrs Morell's chauffeur got £1,000). Six years after Mrs Morell had died, when the Doctor was first interviewed by the police, they found this silver *unused*, in the chest, still wrapped in the original tissue paper.

Counsel for the defence, Geoffrey Lawrence, in his closing speech called the alleged motive ludicrous. 'Ludicrous,' the Judge said in his summing-up, 'is a strong word. But, Members of the Jury, it is a *strong* point.'

Justice Devlin also said that the Doctor might be regarded as a man ' . . . who never in his mind came within the thought of murder'. I go along with that. However grabby and wrong-headed, however unorthodox in his treatment, Dr Adams never dreamt of murdering any of his dear old lady patients.

Nevertheless, except perhaps to the biased general public, the amount of drugs bandied about in the conflicting medical evidence was baffling. The Doctor was extremely fortunate in the *dramatis personae* of his trial. Without the intelligence and good sense of the trial Judge, without the brilliant performance of his defence counsel, without the leaden-minded obstinacy of the prosecution, Dr John Bodkin Adams might well have been convicted.

SYBILLE BEDFORD
London, 1989

CONTENTS

THE FIRST WEEK

THE NURSES

THE SECOND WEEK

THE DOCTORS

CONTENTS

'. . . he has the right to the advantage of the initial incredulity . . .'

MR JUSTICE DEVLIN

THE FIRST WEEK

THE NURSES

DAY ONE

'The trial began at the Central Criminal Court yesterday...'
THE TIMES

THE Judge came on swiftly. Out of the side-door, an ermined puppet progressing weightless along the bench, head held at an angle, an arm swinging, the other crooked under cloth and gloves, trailing a wake of subtlety, of secret powers, age: an Elizabethan shadow gliding across the arras.

The high-backed chair has been pulled, helped forward, the figure is seated, has bowed, and the hundred or so people who had gathered themselves at split-second notice to their feet rustle and subside into apportioned place. And now the prisoner, the accused himself is here – how had he come, how had one missed the instant of that other clockwork entry? – standing in the front of the dock, spherical, adipose, upholstered in blue serge, red-faced, bald, facing the Judge, facing this day. And already the clerk, risen from below the Judge's seat, is addressing him by full name.

There cannot be a man or woman in this court who has not heard it before.

'... You are charged with the murder ...'

And that, too, is expected. It is what all is set for – nobody, today, is here by accident – yet, as they fall, the words in the colourless clerical voice consummate exposure.

'Do you plead Guilty or Not Guilty?'

There is the kind of pause that comes before a clock strikes, a nearly audible gathering of momentum, then, looking at the Judge who has not moved his eyes,

'I am not guilty, my Lord.'

It did not come out loudly but it was heard, and it came out with a certain firmness and a certain dignity, and also possibly with a certain stubbornness, and it was said in a private, faintly non-conformist voice. It was also said in the greatest number of words anyone could manage to put into a plea of Not Guilty. A loquacious man, then, under evident pressure to make himself heard; and how many among those present who do not simply hope that the burden of his plea may be true.

Now what sounds like, but may not quite be, William Makepeace Leader, John Christian Henderson, James Frederick Wright, floats across the court. Men arise from back benches, scurry or shuffle into sight, get themselves into the jury box: two rows, one above the other, of six seated figures cheek by jowl and not a pin to drop between them. Two women are found to be there, side by side in the upper tier. One is in a red coat and hat, the other has jet black hair and a cast of features suggestive of having been reared perhaps under another law. Everybody in this box is, or appears to be, respectable, middle-aged.

The prisoner is still standing. His right to object to any member of his jury has been recited to him by the clerk and he has turned his large, blank, sagging face – a face designed to be jovial – to the jury-box and stares at them with round, sad, solemn eyes. The jurors, one by one, are reading out the oath. It is an old form of words, and it is not couched in everyday syntax. Some approach the printed text with circumspection, some rush it, most come several mild croppers, inexorably corrected – each time – by the usher.

All of this has taken no time at all. A routine dispatched without irrelevancy or hitch between clerk and usher in the well of the court like a practised sheep-herding, while bench and bar stayed aloof. Now counsel for the Crown is on his feet.

Outside in the street, the Old Bailey is sustaining a siege this morning. Police vans and press vans, cameras and cameramen, detective sergeants and C.I.D.s and hangers-on, comings and goings in closed limousines, young men in bowler hats bent double under the weight of papers nudging their way through the crowd, a line of special constables at every door, and thirty extra quarts of milk left for the cafeteria. Here, inside the court, there is more than silence, there is quiet.

A male voice droning: 'May it please your Lordship –', and the case is opened.

A trial is supposed to start from scratch, *ab ovo*. A tale is unfolded, step by step, link by link. Nothing is left unturned and nothing is taken for granted. The members of the jury listen. They hear the tale corroborated, and they hear it denied; they hear it pulled to pieces and they hear it put together again; they hear it puffed into thin air and they hear it back as good as new. They hear it from the middle, they hear it sideways and they hear it straight; they all but hear it backward again through a fine tooth-comb. *But they should never have heard it before.* When they first walk into that court, sit down in that box, they are like people before the curtain has gone up. And this, one is conscious from the first, cannot be so in the present case.

The accused, a doctor, in his fifties, is charged with the murder of a patient six years ago. Leading counsel for the Crown is setting out the prosecution's tale in manageable, spare, slow facts. It is the Attorney-General in person. He is standing in his pew, sheaf of foolscap in hand, a somewhat massive figure, addressing the jury in a full voice. The beginning is a warning. They must try to dismiss from their minds all they may have read or heard of this before.

'This is a very unusual case. It is not often that a charge of murder is brought against a doctor. . . .'

Above on the dais the Judge is listening. Full face and immobile, the robed husk has taken on a measure of flesh and youth. The black cloth and the delicate pair of gloves have been deposited. The face is not the profile; gone is that hint of cunning. This is more than a supremely intelligent face, it is a face marked with intellectual fineness. The Judge sits quite still, in easy absorption. Startling Mandarin hands flower from wide sleeves.

'A word about this doctor. You will hear that he is a doctor of medicine and a bachelor of surgery, that he has a diploma in anaesthetics, holds an appointment as anaesthetist to a hospital and has practised anaesthetics for many years. With his qualifications and experience, you may think perhaps it is safe to assume the Doctor was not ignorant of the effects of drugs on human beings. . . .'

It goes on in a sort of casual boom.

'Now Mrs Morell was an old woman. . . . A widow. . . . A wealthy woman. . . . She left £157,000. . . . She was eighty-one years old when she died in November 1950 in her house at Eastbourne. In 1948, she had a stroke and her left side became paralysed. The Doctor was in charge. She was attended by four nurses; and these nurses will give evidence. They will say they never saw Mrs Morell in any serious pain. The Crown will also call a Harley Street authority. This medical man will tell them that he has formed the opinion that Mrs Morell was suffering from cerebral arterio-sclerosis, in ordinary language [here the Attorney-General lowers his voice a confidential shade], hardening of the arteries. They will hear that for pain to accompany such a condition is most unusual.

'You will hear of large quantities of drugs prescribed for her by the Doctor in the course of months, and supplied to her. One of the questions to be considered in this case will be: why were they given? It is one thing to give an old lady something to help her to sleep, but quite another to prescribe for her large quantities of morphia and heroin. . . .'

Here come detailed figures. The listening mind is pulled up. Figures can be stumbling blocks. These are intended to sound large. They do sound large. Jotted down (roundly), they come to 1629 grains of barbiturates, 1928 grains of Sedormid, 164 grains of morphia, and 139 grains of heroin, prescribed over a period of ten and a half months. One hundred and thirty-nine grains of heroin into ten months make how many grains, or what fraction of a grain, per day – ? And how much is a grain of heroin in terms of what should or could be given – ? To whom, and when, and for what – ?

'. . . You will hear that these drugs if administered over a period result in a serious degree of addiction to them, a craving for them, a dependence on them. . . .' [With weight] 'The Doctor was the source of supply. Did not Mrs Morell become dependent upon him? *Why* were these drugs prescribed to an old lady who was suffering from the effects of a stroke but who was not suffering from pain?'

Through all of this the Doctor has been sitting on his chair in the dock, warder on each side, like a contained explosive. He did not fidget and he did not move, but his face reflected that a remarkable degree of impassivity was maintained by will against an equally high degree of pressure from within. At certain assertions his mouth compressed slowly and hard, and he shook his head, to and fro, almost swinging it, as if prompted by an inner vision that did not correspond to what he had to hear. This head-shaking, which the Doctor repeated throughout his trial, seemed to express sorrow, anger, primness, and exasperation all at once. It was oddly convincing.

'Perhaps,' a hint of complacency in the delivery, 'perhaps you may think that the answer lies in the changes made in her *will*.' Mrs Morell's solicitor, Mr Sogno, will tell them that she made three wills in 1947 and that in none of these wills was there any mention of the Doctor. Then in April 1949 when she had been getting morphia and heroin for some months, the Doctor telephoned to her solicitor saying that she was extremely anxious about her will and wanted to see Mr Sogno that day. So Mr Sogno went to see her and eventually she made another will in which she bequeathed to the Doctor an oak chest containing silver.

'Nearly a year later the Doctor called on Mr Sogno without an appointment and a conversation took place', a sharp look over spectacles at the jury, 'which you may think a very curious one. The Doctor told Mr Sogno that Mrs Morell had promised him her Rolls-Royce in her will and that she now remembered that she had forgotten this, and that she desired to leave him not only the Rolls-Royce car but also the contents of a locked box at the bank, a box which the Doctor said contained jewellery. The Doctor went on to say that though Mrs Morell was very ill, her mind was perfectly clear and she was in a fit condition to execute a codicil. Mr Sogno proposed that they might wait until Mrs Morell's son came at the week-end, but the Doctor suggested that Mr Sogno should prepare a codicil and that the codicil could be executed and later destroyed if it did not meet with Mrs Morell's son's approval. Was not that', another swift look at the jury, 'rather an astonishing suggestion? It showed – did it not? – a certain *keenness*?'

The Attorney-General appears to be an earnest pleader. When he poses a rhetorical question, as he frequently does, it has a dutiful rather than dramatic sound.

Once more Mr Sogno went to see Mrs Morell, and Mrs Morell made another will leaving the Doctor the chest of silver and, if her son predeceased her, the Rolls-Royce and an Elizabethan cupboard. 'Perhaps you might think it significant and sinister that during the period when he was prescribing for her these very substantial quantities of morphia and heroin the Doctor was concerning himself so much about her will and telephoning her solicitor.'

In September of that year the Doctor went away on holiday and his partner looked after Mrs Morell in his absence. She was annoyed with the Doctor for leaving her and executed a codicil revoking her bequests to him.

Here there is one of those pauses which in court are filled not with coughs but an immense rustling of papers. The first exhibit in this case, a photostat of a graph, is being passed round, one up to the Judge, half a dozen to the jury, another copy or two for counsel of the defence. The graph demonstrates the alleged prescriptions by the Doctor.

'... You will see how the prescriptions increased in quantity. ...' During the last thirteen days of Mrs Morell's life the rate of morphia was over three times higher than in any of the preceding months, and the rate of heroin seven and a half times. Why? What had happened to Mrs Morell necessitating these tremendous increases? If she had been in acute pain, heavy doses might have been justified, but she was *not* in acute pain. The nurses will tell you that during her last days she was comatose or semi-conscious. And that brings us back to the question – why did the Doctor prescribe such quantities, such fatal quantities, for which there is no medical justification?' A pause. 'The submission of the Crown is that he did so because he had decided that the time had come for her to die!

'He knew – did he not? – a lot about her will. Whether he knew of the codicil executed while he was on holiday and what happened to it, you may perhaps discover in the course of this trial. The Doctor may have thought she should have no further opportunity for altering her will!'

This leaves a sense of confusion. On the far back benches behind the dock, where the overflow of the irregular press sits squeezed, special correspondents scrawl on their pads and nudge their neighbours. 'But he'd been *cut out* – ?' 'He didn't know.' Someone says just under his breath, 'Bet the old girl told him.' 'That wasn't what he said to the police at Eastbourne.' 'Shsh ...' 'Shshsh. ...'

The Crown must come now to the night of her death. Mrs Morell was lying unconscious. 'The night nurse will tell you she was very weak, except for occasional spasms. [Heavily] She was in a coma. At 10 p.m. the Doctor came and himself filled a 5 c.c. syringe with a preparation –'

The Attorney-General held up an object. It is always slightly startling when an actual utensil of the outside world, not a chart or a document or a photograph of one, appears in a court of law. It does in fact quite often, yet it brings with it a hint of lurid impropriety. It causes what is called a stir; people in the gallery try to stand up and are instantly suppressed.

'The Doctor gave this syringe to the night nurse and told her to inject it into the unconscious woman.' [Tone of doom] 'She did so. The Doctor took the empty syringe and refilled it with a similar quantity – an unusually large quantity on each occasion – and told the nurse to give the second injection to the patient if she did not become quieter. The nurse did not like giving another large injection from this unusually large syringe and later in the evening she telephoned the Doctor. She received her instructions and it was her duty to obey them. She gave the second injection. Mrs Morell gradually became quiet, and at 2 a.m. she died.

'Why were those large injections given to an unconscious woman on the Doctor's orders?

'The prosecution cannot tell you what they were. Mrs Morell may indeed have been a dying woman when they were given. If she was, then the prosecution submits that she was dying from overdoses of morphia and heroin which the Doctor prescribed, and it was murder by him. If, on the other hand, these two injections accelerated her death, it was also murder. The prosecution will submit that the only possible conclusion to which the jury can come is that the Doctor killed her, deliberately and intentionally.'

A slight pause; then before the court has been able to take stock.

'The case for the prosecution does not rest here. On the same day, November 13th 1950, the Doctor filled in a form to secure Mrs Morell's cremation. One question which he had to answer on this form was, "Have you, as far as you are aware, any pecuniary interest in the death of the deceased?" The Doctor's answer in his own writing was, "Not as far as I am aware." Authority was given for Mrs Morell to be cremated.

'Six years later when a detective superintendent from Scotland Yard was making inquiries, he asked the Doctor about this cremation certificate. The Doctor said, "Oh, that was not done wickedly. God knows it wasn't. We always want cremations to go off smoothly for the dear relatives. If I had said I knew I was getting money under the will they might get suspicious, and I like cremations and burials to go off smoothly. There was nothing suspicious really. It was not deceitful."

'But for this false answer on the form, there might not have been a cremation and the prosecution might have been in a position to say how much morphia and heroin there was in the body of Mrs Morell at the time of her death!

'. . . In November 1950, Detective-Superintendent Hannam, with two other detectives, went to the Doctor's house. They went into the surgery and the Doctor was told they had a warrant for a search of the premises for dangerous drugs. . . . The superintendent said, "Doctor, look at this list of your prescriptions for Mrs Morell. There are a lot of dangerous drugs here." Later he asked, "Who administered them?" The Doctor answered, "I did, nearly all. Perhaps the nurses gave some, but mostly me." The superintendent asked, "Were there any of them left over when she died?" and the Doctor replied, "*No, none. All was given to the patient*. Poor soul she was in terrible agony."

'So there you have the Doctor saying that she was in terrible agony, when the nurses will tell you she was comatose and had been comatose for days and had not been suffering real pain.'

And when this had sunk in:

'You will hear that the maximum quantity of heroin which should be prescribed in a period of twenty-four hours is a quarter of a grain. Yet no less than eight grains were prescribed by the Doctor on a single day. The maximum dose of morphia is half a grain. There were ten grains prescribed on the 8th of November, twelve on the 9th, and eighteen on the 11th. The prosecution will call medical authority who will tell you that in their view Mrs Morell could not possibly have survived the administration of these drugs prescribed in her last five days.'

From there the Attorney-General moves forward again to the near present, to 1956 and the inquiry six years after the death, a time-lag surely extraordinary in English justice, and about which we are told nothing.

'... Last November the Doctor went to see Detective-Superintendent Hannam at police headquarters. He asked how the investigation was getting on. The superintendent said, "I am still inquiring into the death of some of your patients, Doctor." The Doctor said, "Which?" and the superintendent answered, "Mrs Morell is certainly one." The Doctor said, "Easing the passing of a dying person is not all that wicked. She wanted to die – that cannot be murder. It is impossible to accuse a doctor."'

Half the court turned to look again at the accused.

'In December, the Doctor was arrested. He was told he would be taken to the police station and charged with the murder of Mrs Morell. He said, "Murder – can you prove it was murder?" Superintendent Hannam said, "You are now charged with murder." And the Doctor said, "I do not think you could prove it was murder – she was dying in any event." As he left the house he gripped the hand of his receptionist and said to her, "I will see you in heaven."

'*She was dying in any event!*' [Decrescendo – businesslike] 'I submit to you that the evidence I and my learned friends will call before you will prove conclusively that this old lady was murdered.' The Attorney-General sits down. The speech has lasted just under two hours.

Instantly a witness is on his way to the stand. A pharmaceutical chemist and what is called a formal witness. His name is given; his address. These will appear tomorrow in *The Times* and perhaps a half dozen national and provincial newspapers. One of the three Crown counsel, a Q.C., swiftly extracts the relevant evidence – the drugs listed by the prosecution were in fact dispensed by Messrs Browne, the chemists, from prescriptions by the Doctor. We learn – if we care to listen – how chemists' books are kept and drugs recorded; we learn how the prosecution's list has been compiled. This witness is followed by another chemist; then a third. The Judge courteously puts a question. It is the first time that we hear him speak, and at once he reveals both grasp and charm. Could it not be stated, he asks, how many grains a 5 c.c. syringe would hold? 12.5 grains, witness replies; that is, if the syringe is quite full. And so, openly, honestly, humbly, the first bare facts are made secure beyond *unnecessary* doubt. It may be dull, it may seem redundant, it certainly is expensive and exacting; it is also gallant and essential, this toiling care to train the light of sequence, truth, and reason on the obvious and minute – justice here is not only seen, it is understood being done. Rigged accusation, fake evidence? a demagogue would meet short shrift. It is thanks to the law's patient production – quixotic almost in its extreme sesquipedalian way – of these routine witnesses: George Albert Church of Greenover Road, Teddington, ironmonger's assistant, who has nothing to gain and nothing to lose and little to fear, that people can rest stolid in their trust that if a man be accused of poisoning or stabbing it must be shown where the poison or a knife came from. It has not always been like this, it may one day be so no longer; even at this time it is not so everywhere. But here and now, while the fourth pharmaceutical chemist is testifying to a preparation of eye-drops, we can allow our minds the luxury to stray.

Court No. 1 at the Old Bailey is a large court as English courts go. It is all the same no more than a large room, and it is packed today. As an auditorium it boasts some drawbacks. For one thing it is cramful of woodwork. Stained oak obstructs foot and eye. Boxes, desks, tables, benches, fitted ingeniously enough, jut at all angles; they hold about two hundred people, and some of them can hear nearly everything and see one thing very well. The witness-box, at conversational distance from the dais, stands in something like the relation of the lectern to the altar; other items bear the stamp of the committee-room, while the benches of the press-box might have come from a Victorian school. The shorthand writer has his own small pen. The dock is something else again. It is like a capacious loose-box, the only space in court that is not jammed, and it is set up plumb in the middle of everything, blocking every view. Yet the sum of these arrangements achieves a satisfying sense of unity. The prisoner can look across the well at the Judge; the Judge sees him. Between them, below, in the small square pit, furrowed by advocates' benches, munitioned from the solicitors' table, the fray takes place.

The jury have the ring-side view; but it is quite impossible for them to look a witness in the face. The public gallery proper is far and high beneath the roof. In court few members of the press or public can see the prisoner and none can see examining counsel *and* his witness at one time; and there are some low rows of seats behind the dock from which no one can see anything at all. All can see the Judge; which does not mean that he can be heard by everyone.

The purpose of a criminal trial is to determine whether a specific act, an event in time, took place or not, or took place in a certain way, to determine in short whether somebody has *done it*. The answer lies with the jury, twelve men and women selected at random within some, nowadays not very stringent, property qualifications. The facts connected with the alleged event are spread in open court by counsel and their witnesses, and re-assembled by the Judge; but it is the jury alone who must come to the conclusion, Yes or No, it was like this or it cannot have been; without their verdict no man in England can be punished for any of the great offences, and their verdict, if it is acquittal, is irreversible.

We now have the bare bones of the prosecution's case. What do they amount to? A woman, eighty-one years old, half paralysed by a stroke, has died. The prosecution says she did not die of age or illness but of drugs. Large doses of drugs, not given at any one time – no poisoner's moment – but drugs prescribed during the last five days of her life without a medical reason. Three questions – at this stage – leap to the mind.

Was the quantity of drugs prescribed actually administered? ('All given to the patient,' the Doctor himself had volunteered, though at a moment when perhaps he hardly had his wits about.)

Was the dosage of these drugs actually fatal, or was it merely – however incomprehensibly or dangerously – very large?

Was there in fact no medical or other reason short of murder for their administration?

On these points, so far, would seem to rest the weight of the whole case, and not on the weak motive or the answer given on a form, or the Doctor's utterances to the police, wild though they may be.

The motive, as presented by the prosecution, is bewilderingly inadequate. Can they be suggesting that a – sane? – man in the Doctor's circumstances would commit murder for the chance of inheriting some silver and an ancient motor-car ironically enough no longer mentioned in the will? Unless some sense or strength can be infused into the motive it must become the sagging point of this unequal web. Yet in a way the motive has already drawn sustenance from an irregular but not secret source; it has waxed big by headlines, by printed innuendo, by items half remembered from the preliminary hearing. There have been published rumours of rich patients, mass poisonings, of legacy on legacy in solid sterling. . . . Everybody knows a bit too much and no one knows quite enough; there is a most disturbing element in this case, extra-mural half-knowledge that cannot be admitted and cannot be kept out.

And so there is a sense of flatness after the prosecution's speech. Was that all? At the very least a tighter case has been expected. There are also some ill-fitted points. The back benches mutter.

'You believe in the unknown quantity in the *unusually large syringe*?'

'Pelion on Ossa.'

'Cheap. Not what you'd expect to get in a British court.'

'Chap's got to put *something* in his case.'

'Shsh. . . '

'Wouldn't you think he could have taken his pick? Widows dying like flies, corpses dug up all over the country . . . '

'Why Mrs Morell?'

'No body.'

'No reasonable gain.'

'Stone cold.'

'Shshsh.'

'*We'll see.*'

The fifth witness for the prosecution – called after the short adjournment: one hour and five minutes for luncheon – is a woman, and a good deal less peripheral. Suddenly the case is under way. Nurse Stronach – stocky, a face of blurred features except for a narrow mouth and strong jaw. By question fitted after question, counsel gets her to put the court in the picture; we have returned to the tortoise from the spectator's hare.

Nurse Stronach was relief nurse to Mrs Morell (in Mrs Morell's own house). Three weeks of night duty in June 1950, one of day duty. Another three weeks of day duty in October. On the Doctor's instructions, she is prompted to tell, Mrs Morell was given a quarter of a grain of morphia every evening. The Doctor came every night.

Counsel [dead-pan, neutral voice]: 'Did you see him do anything with a syringe?'

Nurse Stronach [flatly]: 'He gave her injections.'

'Did you see the Doctor give them?'

[Pursing her mouth] 'We were not allowed in the room.'

'Who forbade you to be in the room?'

'I think it was Mrs Morell's wish that we were not in the room.'

[Making his point] 'You personally did not see the actual injection given, but you did see the Doctor prepare the syringe?'

[Pleased to have this offering] 'Yes, but I could not tell you what it was.'

[Gravely] 'You do not know what the injections which the Doctor gave her were?'

'No, sir, I have no idea.'

'Did the Doctor ever say anything to you about them?'

'He did not tell us.'

[In half tones from the Judge] 'Mr Stevenson, is this perhaps a convenient moment to adjourn?' The usher takes it up; we are on our feet; the Judge has risen, he has his gloves, slides along the bench, is gone. The prisoner has vanished. The pattern is broken up, a crowd of people are making their way, talking, to the door.

Outside it is broad daylight. And one block away we are in London on a warm afternoon in March at 5 p.m.

DAY TWO

Nurse Stronach is still standing in the witness-box. Everybody is in exactly the same place.

'You have told us that the Doctor used to visit Mrs Morell at about 11 p.m. and give her an injection?'

'Yes.'

'That would be after you yourself had given her a quarter of a grain of morphia at 9 p.m.?'

'Yes.'

'And at 11 p.m. Mrs Morell would be fairly dopey and half asleep because of your earlier injection?'

'That is so.'

How would she describe Mrs Morell's general condition? 'She was very weak.' Was there anything else she could tell about her? 'She was getting duller and duller in every way.' Did Nurse Stronach remember anything about her on the last day she was on duty, 2 November, was it not? 'She was rambling and semi-conscious.'

'Did you ever see any signs that she was suffering pain?'

'She did tell me that she had pains, [righteous click] but I considered it neurotic.'

Then it is the turn of the defence. Interest is up. This is the first cross-examination, practically the first time the voice of the defence is heard. What line will there be to take? On the back benches not much love is lost for Nurse Stronach. Something certainly is expected, though nobody then has any idea of how much there is to come.

The name of counsel for the defence is Mr Geoffrey Lawrence, Q.C. Until they have been heard, the figures in counsel's row are but profiles and faces defined under a wig. Distinct and uncontemporary faces, florid or wicked, ascetic, witty, coarse, learned, gay, dimpled, or gnarled; one sees profiles of simian scholars, cupids, and distinguished Jesuits, and the profiles of accomplished sheep.

Mr Lawrence has stood up. He appears a youngish man, slight. *His* profile is a fine one.

'Nurse Stronach, how many patients', the voice is very good, 'do you think you attended since Mrs Morell died?'

'I could not possibly tell you.'

[Suavely] 'A great many?'

'Yes. In private nursing we are in and out constantly.'

Mr Lawrence: 'You have been constantly nursing other patients during the last six or seven years?'

Nurse Stronach: 'Yes.'

'And for what you told my Lord and the members of the jury this morning, you were relying on your memory of events that happened on one case six or seven years ago?'

[Light snap] 'Yes.'

Mr Lawrence [in an easy tone]: 'Just tell me a little about Mrs Morell so far as you were able to know about her case at the time you were there. We have been told she was eighty-one when she died. You knew she was an old lady, did you not?'

'Oh yes.'

'And she had a great many variations in her condition, sometimes up and sometimes down?'

Nurse Stronach: 'That applies to every patient.'

[Still conversational] 'But all the time she was going downhill – generally deteriorating?'

[Off-hand] 'Oh yes.'

'And at the end, as you have said, she was very very weak?'

'Very weak and frail.'

Mr Lawrence: 'And from time to time she had attacks of great irritability?'

'Due to her condition.'

'Against the nurses, was it?'

[Defensive] 'Not only the nurses; other people.'

'It was quite irrational irritability?'

[Satisfied tone] 'It was not normal.'

'It was due to the injuries to the arteries of her brain?'

[Click] 'Not only that.'

Mr Lawrence [covering]: 'That for a start. To what else?'

'I should say a great deal to the amount of drugs she was having.'

[Dryly] 'I thought you were going to say that.'

Now there is an apparent swerve in the line of questioning. She told his learned friend, did she not, that she used to give Mrs Morell an injection of a quarter-grain of morphia? Yes, she did say so. On the Doctor's instructions? Yes. And she never gave anything else by way of an injection? She did not. 'No heroin?' No. 'No Omnopon?' No.

'. . . And the Doctor came in the evening, and he gave a further injection, and he did not tell you what it was? Is that what you said?'

Nurse Stronach [shutting-out tone]: 'I did say so.'

'And you *still* say so?'

'I do.'

There is now a definite sense that counsel is building something. He goes on, treading very lightly. 'I am thinking of what another of the nurses said when she gave her evidence at Eastbourne. She said, "I knew what I was injecting at the time but I cannot remember now; but whatever I gave was written in a book and passed on to the next nurse." ' Mr Lawrence looks at the witness as if asking for further light.

Nurse Stronach seems willing. 'Yes, that is quite correct. We noted down every injection we gave.' She is speaking more freely than she had so far to either of her interrogators, as if now she were on fresh ground. 'It is the usual thing when you are nursing. It is the proper thing to do.'

'All experienced nurses do it?'

'They should do.'

'That is what *you* did?'

'Indeed we did. Every time we gave an injection we wrote it down – what it was, and the time, and signed our names.'

[Gravely now, weight on every word] 'And whatever you wrote in that book would be accurate because it would have been done right at that very moment?'

'It would.'

'*Everything that happened of significance in the patient's illness would have to go down in the book – everything that was of any importance?*'

Nurse Stronach: 'We reported everything, a proper report is written day and night.'

Mr Lawrence [speed again]: 'As distinct from your memory of six years later, these reports would of course be absolutely accurate?'

[Sturdily] 'Oh yes, they would be accurate from each one of us.'

'So that if only we had these reports now we could see the truth of exactly what happened night by night and day by day when you were there?'

'Yes. But you have our word for it.'

Mr Lawrence: 'I want you to have a look at that book please.'

Before anyone quite realizes what is happening there is somewhere a kind of exercise book and it has gone from counsel to the usher and is now in front of Nurse Stronach who at once begins to turn the pages. There is a hovering interval during which the Attorney-General is on his feet but has not said anything, the national Press have leapt their box and are massing by the door, Mr Lawrence hangs fire, and Nurse Stronach is reading. Nobody pays the slightest attention to the Doctor in the dock. Then the Judge says, 'Mr Lawrence, is this one of the exhibits in the case?'

[Hurriedly, staving it off] 'It is not, my Lord, but it will be in due course.' He now turns fully to Nurse Stronach. '*Is this the night report for June 1950? Is it in your handwriting? And is it signed by you?*'

[Lost tone] 'It is.'

[Ringing clear] 'There is no doubt about it? That is the very book of the daily and nightly records kept by the nurses who attended Mrs Morell, and contains your own record?'

[Weakly] 'It is.'

There is the delayed gasp – the Press are through the door – the Attorney-General all but stretches out his hand –

Mr Lawrence: 'I have not finished with it yet.'

The Judge says that if the book were going to be evidence the Attorney-General had a right to see it. Mr Lawrence says it is essential that the books should be identified first. *Books?* (In the general shuffle, all this is rather hard to hear.) Now sure enough another exercise-book is handed up to Nurse Stronach. The first had an orange cover, this one is red. Nurse Stronach agrees that it continues the records kept in the orange book. Then comes a third book, and in this she recognizes her day reports.

Mr Lawrence swings to the Judge. There is something in his fine and compact bearing that suggests the matador holding up the bull's ear. 'At this stage, my Lord, I desire to say that we have the whole of the nurses' reports on this case from June 1949 to November 13th 1950 when Mrs Morell died.'

There ensues one of those brief tripartite mumblings between the Crown, the bench, and the defence. The Attorney-General puts in that he hasn't even seen the alleged nursing reports yet. Finally, a clerk is given leave to open a suitcase, and blue and red sets of ledger-shaped volumes are being dealt all round.

Where did they come from? Why are they produced by the defence? What will they reveal – day-by-day records of allegedly murderous treatment kept by prosecution witnesses at the crucial times? This much is clear, Mr Lawrence must get full marks for audacity.

He is buckling down. In court it is curious how swiftly, seamlessly the dramatic moments subside again into routine. Only the Doctor, one perceives now, still looks smug and pleased. 'Let us look at your first day. When did you come on?'

Nurse Stronach: 'I cannot remember the exact date.'

Mr Lawrence [reassuring, kindly]: 'Of course not. I am not suggesting that you can. You cannot remember after some years, but we can see what you wrote there in the report.'

Nurse Stronach turns over a page.

[Quite sharp suddenly] 'Are you listening to me or are you reading that book?'

[Stolidly] 'I am listening.'

'Am I right in thinking that the nurses made their entries one after the other, the night report following the day report and so on, as each nurse relieved the other?'

'That's how it was done.'

'Now let us go through your entries.' [Reading] ' "June 4th, had milk and brandy (3 drachms). 11 p.m., 1 Sedormid tablet given; milk and brandy repeated; complains of pain and says she has not slept well. 3 a.m., patient awoke perspiring freely, refused to be turned over, said that it hurt her to turn. 6.15 a.m., patient awoke in a temper. Said she had rung the bell and I had not answered it. Said I had left the bed all untidy and that I was a nasty common woman." '

Mr Lawrence puts down the book. 'We have now read your entire entry for that night and two things are clear – first, you did *not* give any injection, and second, the Doctor did *not* visit.'

Nurse Stronach: 'Not according to this.'

'Well, it *is* what you wrote down. Let us look at your entry for June 8th. Again there is no record of any injection and again no record of a doctor's visit, is there?'

'It doesn't say he did not call. It is not proof that he did not call that night.'

'Nurse Stronach! You realize this is a serious case?'

'Indeed, I do.'

'Before you saw this book, you told me that *everything* of importance would have been put down in your record made at the time, didn't you?'

'Yes.'

'And that was the truth?'

'Yes.'

'It is quite clear then that in that first spell of night duty you never recorded yourself as having given any injection at all of any kind, and you never recorded a visit from the Doctor in the evening?'

'Not that I have recorded.'

Mr Lawrence: 'Are you saying that you, a trained nurse – who recorded every drachm of brandy – would not have recorded an injection of a quarter of a grain of morphia if it had been given, or put down a visit from the Doctor if it had occurred?'

'. . . . . .'

[Sharply] 'Do not mutter. We cannot hear you. . . . *Are you saying that you would not have put these down in the book?*'

[More mulish than sheepish] 'No.'

Having got this, Mr Lawrence strides on. 'We will now look at your second period at Mrs Morell's. When you went back on duty in October there was a big difference in her condition from what it was in June?' There was. 'She had deteriorated very much?' She had. 'Let us see what you put down for the day only one month before she died. The entry for 4 p.m. says, "Patient became restless and picking at bedclothes," and this, in your writing, "Hypo injection Omnopon two-thirds given at 4.40 p.m." ' [And now back for more] '*You* gave it – ?'

'Yes.'

[Reasonable; persuasive] 'Do not think I am blaming you, or criticizing you, but you told me earlier this morning that you never had given Mrs Morell any injection except morphia.'

Nurse Stronach: 'I believed that was true.'

[Very bland] 'What this entry shows is that your memory was playing you a trick, does it not?'

'Apparently so.'

'*Obviously* so.'

'It must have done. I cannot remember. It is a long time to remember these things.'

'That' [very pleased] 'is exactly what I suggested to you. It was a long time ago and mistakes of memory can be made. This was one of them.'

The point is driven home; Mr Lawrence moves on. 'Pay attention to this entry – ' And now begin those relentless readings from the nursing books, so strange at first, those pitiful scraps, those close-up admissions to the bedside and helpless hours of an unknown woman who is dead, that were to become as the days went on a kind of merciless obbligato to the case.

' "Patient very thirsty, brandy and water taken. 7.30 p.m., visited by the Doctor. Hypodermic injection: morphia grains one-quarter, heroin grains one-third, Omnopon grains one-third." ' [Looking up] 'So you did record the Doctor's visit? And it is quite clear, on this occasion at any rate, that you knew what his injection was?' [Urging] 'That is true, is it not?' [Back to the book] ' "Patient continued talking and asking for drinks until past midnight – " Notwithstanding the Doctor's injection at 10 o'clock? Is that right? "Very restless. . . . Brain very fuddled, does not know where she is."

' "October 16th, patient very excited. Hypo injection: morphia grains one-quarter, heroin – Omnopon – Slept. Breathing was Cheyne Stokes – " That means alternate periods of heavy breathing and quite shallow breathing, doesn't it? and is quite typical of elderly people suffering from stroke and in the last stages of senile deterioration?'

Nurse Stronach [vaguely as if she had not followed]: 'Yes.'

Mr Lawrence: 'You are not feeling well?'

[Semi-bristle] 'I am all right, thank you very much.'

It is well past noon. Whatever else Mr Lawrence may require of his witness, he expects her full attention. One wonders – where does it begin, the road that leads into the witness-box? The police call; one talks, one is reluctant or one does one's best, perhaps one volunteers; details come flooding back, one realizes one knows something of significance, or thinks one does; another interview; a statement made; and there one is called for the prosecution. The day is a long way off. And first there is the evidence before the magistrates, the inspector has said it's nothing, one knows a face or two in court, no one presses very hard, the defence shows no claws. . . . The great day is there. Well, one's only come to do one's duty. London. The Central Criminal Court. One's picture in every evening paper. Waiting. One's name is called. And there one stands in fur-tipped hat and coat and everything is quite different. The daze wears off. . . . The jury doesn't look like much, the Judge looks kind (one hardly likes to look at the accused), the Q.C. is ever so considerate: answers trip off, it's easy. And *then* comes the cross-examination.

' "October 20th, patient was stripping the bedclothes. Complained of pain across the forehead. General condition very low." ' Look from book to witness. 'No injection; *no* visit from the Doctor.

' "October 22nd, patient had a good night on the whole. Seems brighter. Breakfast: boiled egg, bread and butter, bramble jelly, 2 cups of tea." No injection and no doctor's visit.

' "October 23rd, very restless and her speech indistinct. Water, 6 ozs, taken indifferently. Cried at intervals. Asked for fruit jelly." *Again* – no injection.

' "5.30 a.m., asked for a drink and was given some milk-and-soda. 7 a.m., persuaded to take a Sedormid tablet with Malvern water, but tried to push the glass away. . . .

' "A quiet night, but patient in a confused state of mind. . . .

' "Had a very quiet morning. Special injection given by the Doctor. Lunch at 1 p.m., Allenbury's, 10 oz., taken. 2 p.m., became very restless, talking at random . . .

' "Seen by the Doctor in the morning. Special injection given.

Patient depressed and sullen. Cried. Supper at 6.30 p.m., tomato soup, croutons, Malvern water, jelly taken . . .

' "October 31st, Doctor's instructions omit morphia and Omnopon. Instead give at night one-half heroin, and one-third during the day, s.o.s. . . . " '

Mr Lawrence [putting the book down]: 'We have now been through the whole of your records for that time, we have not found a single instance where you gave the injection of one-quarter grain of morphia by itself you were talking about. And you recorded only one or two visits by the Doctor, and then we find you knew exactly what injection was given. You told my learned friend this morning that on your last day with Mrs Morell she was "rambling and semi-conscious". Do you remember saying that?'

[Shut-faced] 'I do.'

'We have your own record of that day. Let me read it to you. You wrote down what this semi-conscious woman consumed for lunch. "A small quantity of partridge, a small quantity of celery, a small quantity of pudding, and a small quantity of brandy-and-soda." That is not the picture of a semi-conscious woman, is it?'

[Low voice] 'She wouldn't have been having much, these would have been quite small quantities. . . . '

Mr Lawrence: 'I did *not* say that she had an *enormous meal* of partridge and celery and pudding and brandy-and-soda. I said' [ringing it through the court] 'I said she had *a small* quantity of partridge, *a small* quantity of celery, *a small* quantity of pudding, and *a small* quantity of brandy-and-soda. Let us face this, Nurse Stronach; it is another complete trick of your memory to say that the day you left Mrs Morell was either rambling or semi-conscious?'

'I have nothing to say.'

'*You have nothing to say?*'

'No.'

And soon, the parting shot. 'You also told my learned friend that Mrs Morell was always very dopey and half-asleep when the Doctor gave her that night injection because you had already given her one. That turns out to be quite inaccurate too?'

This time something goes wrong with the answer. 'Well, since the day nurse had already given her an injection – '

[Cutting in] 'Your evidence was that *you* gave it.'

'So I understood, but I did not do so.'

Mr Lawrence sits down. It has been beautifully done, the sequence and control of details, the moods of tone – how the witness's credit with the jury must have been impaired – yet at times it also felt like skating. In the back, an American agency-man writes on his pad, 'The nurse being all mixed up doesn't mean the old lady didn't get plenty of dope from whoever it was.' It is a point. Nurse Stronach had said she gave morphia and morphia only; it has turned out that what she gave was morphia mixed with heroin and Omnopon.

Luncheon adjournment. Groups drift and form. There is the basement cafeteria in the building, there is the choice of the three pubs across the road.

'Tom Brown, *Iowa Globe*.'

'Bob White of *X.C.Y.*'

'*Sydney Chronicle*.'

'*Lui c'est le Figaro, moi je suis Paris-Presse*.'

'*Il Corriere . . .*'

'*Il Giornale . . .*'

'*Prensa . . .*'

'Fellow over there is *Life*.'

'*Hamburger Anzeiger . . .*'

'*Uinjenwaarten . . .*'

The regulars of the national Press keep themselves to themselves, and only the very brave dare go near the Press-room. The French and some of the other Latins eat in the cafeteria, the Anglo-American element goes across the road. The Central Europeans tend to vanish beyond Ludgate Hill into coffee places known only to themselves.

Nurse Stronach's re-examination is by the Attorney-General and quite brief. The prosecution so far has had no time to read the evidence in the nursing books. So they are throughout this day on most uncertain ground. The object, generally, of a re-examination is to repair and minimize such damage as the cross-examination may have wrought upon a witness and his story. The questioning here gives an impression of fairness and seems to show a genuine wish to know where everybody is, and a wish to leave ill alone. No attempt is made to rehabilitate the witness's memory. It goes on these lines:

Some of the nursing reports refer to a special injection given by the Doctor, did she know at any time what this injection was?

Nurse Stronach: 'I cannot remember. I did know, but I cannot remember.'

The Attorney-General: 'I want you to be absolutely frank about this and if you have any doubt about it, do say so for this is a very serious matter. To the best of your recollection now, were you at any time informed by the Doctor what this special injection was?'

'No, not by the Doctor.'

'Were you ever informed by anyone?'

'I think one of the nurses told me at the time, but I don't know, I think they were for a special purpose.'

They leave it at that. When the Crown has finished, the Judge begins to speak. He makes a half-turn towards the witness-box and pleasantly, conversationally, moving his fine hands, he says he would like to know a little more about how the drugs came into the house. Did the Doctor ever write the prescriptions in her presence?

Nurse Stronach: 'He often did.'

The Judge: 'Was that because someone had told him that the supply was running out, or because he found out himself?'

'He would probably ask and we would tell him how the drugs were going.'

'He would write out a fresh prescription and would give it to the nurses?'

'Yes, and we would give it to the chauffeur, Price, who took it to the chemist. And when he brought them, they would be taken in by the cook; she would bring them to the dining-room to the nurse on duty who would put them away. The nurses had charge of the locked cupboard in the dining-room where the drugs were kept. If the Doctor wanted drugs from the cupboard he would ask for them and we would produce the key; but he usually had his own drugs from his bag.'

The Judge thanks her, and Nurse Stronach steps from the box. It is now a quarter to three. She is followed at once by another nurse, the sixth prosecution witness, who has been waiting her turn outside the court. Sister Mason-Ellis was with Mrs Morell in 1949 and again in 1950 up to the time of her death. She is a thin, rather pale, tallish, fairish woman, dressed in beige, apparently not strong. Unlike Nurse Stronach, one would never take her for a nanny, and, also unlike Nurse Stronach, she is married.

The Attorney-General [as if reading out the question]: 'Sister Mason-Ellis, when the Doctor visited Mrs Morell were you present in the room?'

[Low voice; diffident] 'I was not.'

[Still as if reading, and reading slowly] 'The Doctor was alone with Mrs Morell?'

'Yes, we were asked to leave.'

'That happened every time the Doctor was there?'

'I think so.'

'Did you yourself see the Doctor give an injection to Mrs Morell?'

'I could not answer that.' [Trailing off] 'It is so long ago.'

'Could you please try to keep your voice up? What was her condition in November?'

Sister Mason-Ellis: 'That was six years ago – ' [distressed] 'I could not honestly and truthfully answer about her then . . . '

'Could you tell us something about her general condition?'

'It was so long ago. Honestly – it was six years. . . . '

Now Mr Lawrence has his try. She looked after Mrs Morell at intervals, he begins, because the nurses kept on changing, 'and some of these changes were brought on by Mrs Morell's own bad temper?'

Sister Mason-Ellis: 'That is true.'

Mr Lawrence: 'She was a very difficult woman to nurse?'

[Vividly] 'Yes, she was.'

'But one always had to remember that she had a stroke and couldn't get out of bed and had to be lifted into her wheel-chair? And in addition to her physical disability she showed signs of cerebral irritation?'

'Yes.'

'So right from the start, when you went there in August 1949, she was under routine sedation?'

'Yes, I think so.'

'The entry you made on August 27th was your first as a nurse to Mrs Morell. You had then given a hypodermic injection of a quarter of a grain of morphia and a third of a grain of heroin. And that was the routine standard dose at that time that she had every night?'

'It must have been.'

More passages from the nursing books. 'I think we shall find that for months and months and months that routine sedation went on without any alterations?'

'Yes, so far as the reports are concerned.'

Obliged to tie this up once more, 'I can take it that what you wrote in the reports over your signature is what *actually happened*?'

'Oh, yes.'

'And now let us look at one of your entries for December. You see what you had to encounter on that day. "Patient very disturbed this afternoon. Shouting and quite hysterical for about an hour. Another outburst in the evening." That was the sort of temper poor Mrs Morell displayed from time to time?'

'It was.'

'Now in a case where a patient has a stroke involving brain irritation, is it not an essential part of the treatment that she should have sleep and quiet at night, if she can get it?'

'Oh, I agree.'

Mr Lawrence, among other things, must have kept his eye upon the clock, for it is after such a point that the Judge tenders his convenient moment. We adjourn. The jury, too, goes home – by another door, down other stairs – unapproachable, unapproached. What may be their reflections? Less inhibited, on the public stairway the voices buzz. 'Lawrence's doing fine – Remember, the defence hasn't got to *prove* anything, just shoot a lot of holes, pump 'em full of doubt – Heroin for bad temper, that's a new one. Well, for all we know – '

DAY THREE

10.31 A.M. The court has barely settled down. Mr Lawrence, on the floor, untouchable and stern, plunges.

'Last night,' he flings at Sister Mason-Ellis, who rather wanly stands before him, 'last night after you left the witness-box you were talking to Nurse Stronach and Nurse Randall, weren't you?'

At once everybody is feeling most uncomfortable.

Sister Mason-Ellis [lightly]: 'That's right, yes.'

'The three of you were talking in the hall of this building, weren't you?'

'Yes, we were.'

Nurse Randall is the next witness listed for the prosecution and has been glimpsed sitting about the hall knitting.

'The three of you', Mr Lawrence makes them sound a pack, 'travelled together from Victoria to the coast?'

'Yes, we did.'

[Ringing] 'With the evening papers in front of you – reading together the report of this case?'

[Keeping her voice neutral] 'That's right.'

'*And discussing it together?*'

One does not see why Sister Mason-Ellis has not fled into the dock. Instead, she qualifies quite sensibly, 'Discussing what was in the newspapers, yes.'

Mr Lawrence does not turn on the Press box. 'All three of you travelled back to London this morning by the 8.04 train – again in the same train – this time with the morning papers in front of you and discussing this case together?'

'Yes.'

[Very slow] 'Did one or the other of you say something to this effect, "Don't you say that or you will get me into trouble"?'

Sister Mason-Ellis: 'I cannot answer that.'

'*You cannot answer it?*'

'No.' Sister Mason-Ellis begins to appear a heroine.

'Perhaps I did not make my question clear. Let me try again.' [Loud and clear] 'In the course of your discussion in the train this morning did one or the other of you – it may have been you, it may have been Nurse Stronach or Nurse Randall – say words like these, now listen: "Don't you say that or you will get me into trouble"?'

[Very distressed. Shallow voice] 'Yes, I think one of them did say that, but which one I'm afraid I cannot say.'

'Was it *you*?'

[Full voice] 'Oh no.'

'Then it was either Nurse Stronach who had already given evidence; or Nurse Randall who has not yet been called.' [Quick whip] 'Which of those two was it?'

[Looking about her] 'Must I answer that?'

The Judge at once: 'Yes.'

[Faintly] 'Then it was Nurse Randall.'

Mr Lawrence [not letting up]: '*And to whom did she say it?*'

'She spoke to both of us.'

'Surely, to *you*?'

'Yes.'

'*You*, as you know, are not only in the middle of giving your evidence,' [chord] 'but in the middle of being cross-examined by myself on behalf of the Doctor.' [Lashing out] '*What* was it she told you not to say?'

Quite a pause. 'I really cannot remember;' [Genteelly] 'I was not terribly interested if I may say so.'

Mr Lawrence [taking none of that]: 'I am *not* asking you, Sister Mason-Ellis, about something that happened six years ago. What were you talking about *this morning* when Nurse Randall said, "Don't you say that or you will get me into trouble"?' Nurse Randall can hardly have said those words in quite that voice.

[Unhappily] 'About the drugs.'

'And *what was it* you were not to say?'

'There's been a little confusion – You see, the drugs were kept in a drawer, not in a cupboard, and there was no key.'

Mr Lawrence: 'Did you know that Nurse Stronach told my Lord yesterday that these drugs were kept in a *locked* cupboard of which the nurses kept the key and produced the key when the Doctor wanted to go to the cupboard?' [Looking at her] 'Did she tell you that?'

'I believe I saw it in the paper. We did not have any key at any time I know of.'

'You saw that in the paper and so far as your recollection goes, it was untrue? If there were no cupboard there was no locking and the whole of it was untrue, wasn't it?'

'Yes. That's why we were discussing it.'

[Letting her have it] 'That is why you – in the middle of your evidence – with the Doctor on a charge of murder – were discussing the case with a witness who you knew had given wrong evidence? Is that right?'

'I did not give the evidence.'

'You *knew* Nurse Stronach had given these answers?'

'Not until I saw it in the paper.'

'You knew it then because you read it?'

'Yes.'

There is more to come. 'When you were sitting in the hall of this building last night and before you left to catch your train home, were you not told by Superintendent Hannam that you were not to talk to each other?'

This new proof of Mr Lawrence's omniscience must be most bewildering.

'Yes.'

'And notwithstanding that, you all go down in the train together and come up again together this morning and talk it over amongst yourselves?'

'From the newspapers ...'

'Did you talk to her about the note-books?'

'Not the contents. I just said I was glad they had been found.'

Mr Lawrence [complete change of manner: aloof, reasonable]: 'Did she agree with you?'

'She didn't really answer me.'

'*You* are glad they have been found.'

[Looking up] 'I am.'

[Rational approval] 'For this reason – that these books tell the truth? And that we can only get at the truth by looking at these contemporary records?'

[Meek voice] 'Exactly.' Does Sister Mason-Ellis believe herself forgiven, or is she past noticing?

There is only a slight pause; Mr Lawrence picks up his copy of the nursing reports and resumes where he left off yesterday.

' "1950. May 4th, Mrs Morell rather trying this afternoon. Worried about blankets on her bed, one being shorter than the other. Refused to be placated until all store blankets, including those on beds, been presented to her." You mean to say she had to have every blanket in the house brought to her room?'

'That's right.'

' "May 11th, very difficult and depressed from 3.30 to 5 p.m. Very weepy and accused me of leaving her alone the whole afternoon to die. Told me I should be dismissed when the Doctor returned. . . . " Evidently he was away on holiday?'

'Yes.'

'At this period she was being looked after by his partner, Dr Harris?'

'Yes.'

It is obviously a fact of much importance. For the present it is shelved. Dr Harris did not give evidence before the Eastbourne magistrates.

' " . . . I refused to look after her and did nothing but sit down while I was on duty. Wished she was dead and that she knew a doctor who would put her to sleep forever." ' Mr Lawrence [delighted with this]: 'Wished she was dead and that she knew a doctor who would put her to sleep forever! She was attended by the Doctor and by Dr Harris for months, and there she is still wishing . . . '

Sister Mason-Ellis [earnestly]: 'I don't know to whom she was referring.'

'Now we come to the 25th of May when there was a little trouble about her teeth. . . .

' "May 30th, brighter this a.m. Looked at television. Cytamen injection given by the Doctor." That is a vitamin preparation? So there is no doubt what these morning injections given by the Doctor were?'

'Yes, when they were written down.'

Mr Lawrence [incredulous]: 'As a trained nurse you would not have put anything down that was not accurate?'

[Sincerely] 'That would have been shocking.'

' "June 18th, had an 'outburst'. Called me a slum woman and a brute. Has been very argumentative over everything since. 3 p.m., very hysterical re Bessie and the sugar ration, throwing off the bedclothes and beating the bed in anger." Let us get this clear – that was obviously a bad outburst that afternoon, and this occurred without any increase at all in the drugs she had been having month after month?'

'Quite.'

'Let us look at September 24th.' Every time a witness is invited to do this, the members of the jury, too, obediently turn the pages of their copies of the nursing books (one copy to every two jurors), and there is a short wait. The Doctor also has his copy. ' "Breathing rapid, at times 34." That means 34 breaths a minute?'

'Yes, that was very fast.'

Mr Lawrence: 'When people are under the influence of morphia and heroin their breathing tends to get slow, does it not?'

'Yes, slow.'

[Driving it home] 'And this was just the opposite? And quite typical of the closing stages of cerebral irritation?' Yes. 'And this time it was plain that she was rapidly going downhill?' Yes. 'And the Doctor thought that she ought to have some sleep?' Yes.

At this stage, Mr Lawrence offers Sister Mason-Ellis a chair, which she accepts. It is lifted into the box and she sits down at once.

Now they must come to her entries for Mrs Morell's last days. 'On November 3rd the Doctor ordered one Sedormid tablet only to be given on waking and nothing more until after the visit of her son that afternoon as he wanted her to be clear mentally. "Patient very lachrymose and sullen. Did not want to see her son and cried most of the visit. Later patient became hysterical. Said I was trying to kill her. Supper at 6.30, soup, brandy-and-water, jelly taken."

' "November 8th – " this is five days before she died – "sat in a chair for eight minutes, then returned to bed."

' "November 9th, asked for chicken soup and had a cupful, also queen's pudding and ice-cream. Asked for sherry in her soup and ate half a baked apple."

' "November 12th." What is the first word you have written here?'

Sister Mason-Ellis [reading from her copy]: ' "Awake – " '

Mr Lawrence [taking over]: ' "Awake, but quiet. Half a glass of milk and brandy 3 drachms taken." It is quite obvious from that report – which as we know is the fountain of truth – that she was not in a coma?' One is aware of what Mr Lawrence is trying to do, he is trying to lay the image evoked by the prosecution's opening speech, the image of injection after heavy sedative injection pumped into the body of an unconscious woman.

Sister Mason-Ellis [hedging; the story of the coma may quite likely have been started by the nurses]: 'Well, not according to my report . . . '

Mr Lawrence [rising note]: 'More than once you have agreed with me that these reports are the places where the truth is to be found. You do not want to go back on that now, do you?'

'Not at all.'

'So when you write "awake" on the last afternoon before she died, she must have been awake?'

'She must have been.'

[Conclusively] 'Therefore she could not possibly be in a coma.' And having got there, he turns it off at once. Now to mop up some (presumably) ancillary matters. Where exactly, after all, did they keep those drugs? They were kept, Sister Mason-Ellis says, in a drawer in the sideboard, but the drugs in use were kept on a tray. 'We call it the hypodermic tray; it was kept in the dining-room – we nurses usually sat there – covered with a towel.'

'Sister Mason-Ellis, after Mrs Morell died, did her son write to you?'

[Standing up again] 'He wrote and thanked me for what I'd done and sent me a little present that Mrs Morell wished me to have. It was not in the will.'

'Do you mind if I ask you what it was?'

'A cheque for fifty pounds.'

Sister Mason-Ellis has been cross-examined for nearly four

hours, her re-examination takes twenty minutes. The Attorney-General tries to make three points. The first is that Mrs Morell was not suffering any serious pain. Taking a leaf from the defence's books, he asks, 'Would you ever wittingly leave anything important out of the nursing reports?'

'Of course not.'

'There is *no* entry by you recording Mrs Morell as suffering severe pain?'

'She did not appear to have any pain at all as far as I am concerned.'

The Attorney-General [intoning]: 'If she had appeared to be suffering any severe pain, would you have entered that in your notes or not?'

'Most certainly.'

[Making it a right-and-left] 'Are morphia and heroin pain-killers?'

'They are.'

And the second point, 'Throughout the whole of the period you were attending Mrs Morell, she was having at first morphia and heroin, and later morphia, heroin, and Omnopon?'

'She was.'

[Slowly] 'Have you ever before for any other doctor given injections of morphia and heroin mixed?'

'I cannot remember that. Heroin is not often used.'

[Very slowly and deliberately] 'Have you, in your experience as a nurse, ever administered them as a routine injection given every evening?'

[Unqualified] 'No.'

The third point ends in a draw. The Attorney-General reminds Sister Mason-Ellis of her own entry on the day of the son's visit when the Doctor had instructed that Mrs Morell was to be given no sedation as he wanted her to be mentally clear. 'So the administration of drugs *would* affect the state of her mind?'

'Yes, it would.'

'It has been suggested by my learned friend repeatedly that this muddled state and confusion was consistent with senile decay? Can you say whether it was or not?'

Sister Mason-Ellis: 'Well, it was both really.'

(On the back benches they mutter, 'One step backwards, two steps sideways, we'll be here next month at this rate. . . . ')

'If they couldn't sew it up any better than that, they shouldn't have brought the damn case at all.'

'*Don't say that or you will get me into trouble.*'

'There's some private eye behind you.'

'Shsh.'

'You don't think the defence actually had them *followed*?'

'I've seen *you* with the newspaper in front of you – discussing this case.'

'Good old days: lock up the jury, lock up the witnesses, no drink, no food, no light, no fire.'

'They didn't do that?'

'Worse.'

'Police state!'

'*Private* police.'

'Shshsh.'

'Didn't amount to much though at the end, did it? I mean, didn't do these nurses any good and all that – but it didn't clear the Doctor or anything?'

'*No key* to that sideboard. *Bothering* to *lie* about it.'

'Those drugs were open to anyone . . . '

'Ah, yes.'

The Judge has his word with the witness; attention is riveted again. He wants to know more about how the injections were recorded in the nursing books. There is a world of difference between questions by a judge and questions by the advocates. Advocates have to try to bring out certain answers and to keep others covered; a judge asks to learn what happened. If the Doctor himself gave an injection, he asks, how would the nurses know what to put down? Sister Mason-Ellis explains that they would know from the amount of tablets missing from their stock. 'We kept a record of all dangerous drugs. We must always put down the amount of drugs we use in case we are asked.'

The Judge: 'What sort of a record?'

'We wrote down on bits of paper the number of tablets we took out of the tubes.'

'Bits of paper?'

'Strips of paper, anything we could find to write on.'

'What were the drugs like on the tray?'

Sister Mason-Ellis: 'They were very small tablets in very thin tubes like a straw you drink from.'

'*Tablets?*'

'You dissolve them in water, distilled water, before making an injection.'

The Judge: 'Now if you had been out of the room, then came back and the Doctor told you the wrong figure of tablets, you would have discovered it sooner or later?'

'We would have; but usually the Doctor had his own drugs from his own bag, and his own syringe.'

'And on those occasions you just relied on what he told you?'

'Yes.'

'One more thing, Sister Mason-Ellis, when you had to be outside the dining-room, the Doctor would be alone with the tray and the drugs?'

'Not always. I would take the hypodermic tray with me. When I was with the patient I had the tray with me in the bedroom; it was kept on the window-ledge.'

The Judge: 'You took the tray with you wherever you went? Is that part of the regular routine?'

'It should be; and it's my routine wherever I am.'

The Judge says, 'Thank you very much, Sister Mason-Ellis.'

One expected now to see Nurse Randall (of the indiscretions in the train), who was Mrs Morell's regular nurse and the Crown's chief nursing witness; instead, an old gentleman stepped rather gingerly into the box. He used to be a medical referee at Brighton Crematorium, and it was he who had dealt with Mrs Morell's cremation form. He has an air of What's-that? when asked something and takes his time over the answers.

Junior counsel for the Crown makes him explain intelligibly to the court that before permission can be given to cremate, a form known as Form B has to be filled in by the doctor who attended the patient whose body is to be cremated. There is also a Form C which has to be filled in by an outside doctor, and a Form F filled in by the authorities. On Form B the attending doctor has to certify that death was not due to 'violence, poison, privation, or neglect'.

Counsel: 'I want to draw your attention to Question 4. "Have you, as far as you are aware, any pecuniary interest in the death of the deceased?" Answer, "Not so far as I am aware." Dr Walker, if you had any doubt as to the accuracy of that answer, would you have signed the authority for the cremation to proceed?'

Witness [uncertainly]: 'I think not.'

Counsel: 'Would you mind reading us out the whole of the completed form?'

Witness settled down to do so. ' "Having attended deceased before death and having seen and identified the body after death, I give the following answers to the questions set out below.

' "Date and hour of death – 13th Nov. at 2 a.m.;

' "What was the immediate cause of death – Cerebral thrombosis;

' "What was the mode of death – Coma." '

Counsel now produces a number of forms; the witness identifies them, and counsel thanks him.

It is Mr Lawrence's turn. 'You are aware that at the bottom of Form B there is a space?'

Witness puts on his spectacles again.

Mr Lawrence: 'This space is left for the doctor to add anything he likes? But he is not bound to add anything if he does not wish to?'

'.....'

[Louder] 'The doctor is not obliged to enter anything into that space, if you follow me, Dr Walker?'

'Oh, quite.'

'And into this space, as you see, the Doctor has put the addresses of the three nurses who attended Mrs Morell?'

'.....'

'So anybody reading this form would have all the material information supplied by the Doctor?'

'.....'

'They could go at once to any of the nurses – could they not? – and ask them questions about Mrs Morell's case?'

[Dully] 'They could have.'

[Insisting] '*All* the names and addresses were supplied by the Doctor?'

'Quite.'

'And, independently, a Dr Fox has stated on Form C that he had questioned the Doctor and that he had questioned one of the nurses alone, and he, too, has certified the cause of death as cerebral thrombosis?'

'Quite.'

'And Dr Fox knew of no reason to suspect she died a violent or unnatural death, or a sudden death?'

'. . . . .'

'Or died in circumstances which required an inquest?'

'. . . . .'

'Dr Walker, *you* would not have authorized the cremation unless you had this confirmatory certificate by Dr Fox?'

'What?'

Mr Lawrence repeats the question.

'Oh, quite.'

The Judge says something, but dearly though one should have liked to hear them, both question and answer are inaudible and the witness steps down.

And now there is Nurse Randall. As she takes the oath – a stocky, opaque figure diffusing compressed energy – there is a hallucinatory moment when one believes that Nurse Stronach has come back. Soon, however, Nurse Randall establishes her own identity.

She had been, we hear, with Mrs Morell for nearly two years. The Attorney-General begins with what has become his stock question, Had she ever injected a mixture of morphia, heroin, and Omnopon on the instruction of any other doctor?

'No, I don't think I have.'

[Intoning] 'Have you ever on the instruction of any other doctor given a *routine* injection of morphia and heroin?'

'No.'

And, 'At any time while you were nursing Mrs Morell, did you see any sign that she was suffering from severe pain?'

'Not severe pain. There was stiffness because she was unable to walk.'

'Nurse Randall, on the Doctor's visits, when he was alone

with Mrs Morell, did the Doctor ask you for anything?'

'He did.'

'What did he ask you for?'

'The Doctor always asked for a glass of hot water.'

Then came the nursing books. Compliant rustling in box and dock.

The Attorney-General: 'You recorded in this night report that she became breathless and rather collapsed. What did you put this down to?'

Nurse Randall: 'I put this down to the heroin not suiting her and I told the Doctor so.'

'Did he agree with you?'

'He told me he did not think that the patient's condition had anything to do with the heroin.'

There has now emerged a pattern in the prosecution's leading of the nurses' evidence. Over and over, the questions seek to implant three distinct points:

That a routine injection of morphia and heroin is something unusual, outlandish, unheard of, therefore suspect.

That Mrs Morell was not in pain. (The defence meets this with *their* stock point that the medication was justified by the restlessness.)

That the nurses were ordered out of the patient's room during the Doctor's visits, thus sinister opportunity. (The defence harps on this having been on Mrs Morell's request.)

Presently they come to the last week. On November 6th, Nurse Randall gave half a grain of heroin at 1 a.m. and again at 1.55 a.m., and another half-grain at 7.40 a.m. 'In your report you added the words, "On the Doctor's orders". Why did you write that?'

Nurse Randall: 'I think it was because the 1.55 a.m. injection followed so closely on the other one.'

'All this time she was going downhill quickly. Larger quantities were given. By November 8th she had half a grain of heroin *and* half a grain of morphia and millesimal of atropine at night, and an hour later she was still awake and given an identical injection. She had no sound sleep, and by early morning she was getting irritable and aggressive and a third injection of the same drugs was given.

'The next night, we have the same pattern. She slept until 1 a.m., then became wide awake and was given a half-grain each of morphia and heroin with atropine. At 4.30 a.m. she was fidgety and talkative and the same injection was repeated.'

(The correspondent of an Italian illustrated paper leans over to an English free-lance, 'You know that atropine is a kind of antidote?' 'Is it? How curious.' 'They should bring that out.' 'Trust Mr Lawrence.')

'On the 10th, she had an injection of hyperduric morphia by the Doctor at about 10 p.m. – '

As one is trying to follow the sequence of these nights, one realizes that one never hears a round-the-clock report of a full day. Each nurse can only be examined on her own spell of duty. So after each early morning we go straight on to the Doctor's next evening injection 'at about 10 p.m.'. It is difficult to interfile, to place these choppy nights of deep drugging and sharp wakefulness between the corresponding days of jelly and queen's pudding and 'asked for sherry in her soup' recorded by Sister Mason-Ellis.

' . . . And the Doctor leaves instructions "To have heroin *one grain hourly* if necessary". That was a new development, wasn't it?'

Mr Lawrence is on his feet before Nurse Randall can give her answer. 'I must ask the Attorney-General not to lead in that form.'

The Attorney-General [remaining urbane]: 'I will put the question in another way – had you had any similar instructions before to give *one grain* of heroin *hourly* if necessary?'

Nurse Randall: 'No.'

'And at 4 a.m. that night you gave the one grain of heroin? "Gives a sharp cry at every touch; twitching more pronounced." Later she dozed off, but soon became fidgety again, and was given *another whole grain* of heroin. "7.30 a.m., awoke very restless and confused. 8 a.m., visited by the Doctor; injection of hyperduric morphia given." ' [Putting down the book] 'Can you say whether or not during those last nights of her life she was receiving more injections than in any previous period you had been nursing her?'

Nurse Randall: 'I should say she was having more.'

[With weight] 'Did the Doctor tell you *why* to give heroin one grain hourly if necessary?'

'No.'

The few reasonably incontrovertible facts about the Doctor are that he is fifty-eight years old; was born and brought up – a Methodist – in Ulster Ireland; lost his father when he was fifteen and his only brother at eighteen; qualified at Belfast at twenty-two; came to Eastbourne at twenty-three, practised, prospered, and remained. He never married. Most of his adult life was spent with his mother (a temperance worker) until her death some years ago. He taught Sunday school and was chairman of the local Y.M.C.A.

The Attorney-General: 'On the night of the 11th we see that the Doctor went back to giving her half a grain each of morphia and heroin. At 1 a.m. she was again fidgety and talkative and this time the injection was half a grain of hyperduric morphia and a whole grain of heroin. At 3 a.m. she was still awake, and at 3.40 a.m. she was given another grain of heroin. "Patient has not had a very good night. No sleep up till 7 a.m. Talkative and very jerky. Taken no nourishment. Becomes violently agitated."

'And the report of November 12th – her last night – goes, "Patient very weak and restless. 9.30 p.m., paraldehyde 5 c.c. given intravenously by the Doctor." '

Paraldehyde? No household word exactly, but it is a name put on the prosecution's large unknown quantity. There is a measure of curiosity as to how this is going to be met.

' " . . . 11.30 p.m., very restless. No sleep. 12.30 a.m., seems a little quieter; appears asleep. 2 a.m., passed away quietly." ' Now comes an unexpected question. 'Did you perceive any jerks?'

Nurse Randall: 'Yes, they were very bad.'

The Attorney-General: 'How bad? Could you give an indication?'

'They were so bad I could not leave her, and they almost jerked her out of bed.'

'Have you ever seen jerks as bad as that in any other patient?'

'Never.'

(Here one of the agency men passes a note along his row. 'Jerky spasms are a symptom of opiate poisoning.')

The Attorney-General: 'When this 5 c.c. injection was given what was her condition?'

Nurse Randall: 'She was not conscious. She might have been semi-conscious.'

The Attorney-General: 'I want you to tell the court how this injection came to be made. The Doctor came? What happened when he came?'

'She was very jerky.'

'What did the Doctor do?'

'I think he was trying to do something to make her quiet for the night as I was alone.'

[Droning] 'Where was the injection prepared?'

There is a sense of the Attorney-General going after something we do not know about.

'In the dining-room.'

'Whose syringe was it?'

[Gulping] 'It must have been the Doctor's, it was the first time a 5 c.c. syringe had come into the house. . . . '

'Who prepared it?'

'The Doctor.'

'Who injected it?'

'I think the Doctor did.'

'And when it was given, what did the Doctor do then?'

Nurse Randall: 'He refilled the syringe and gave it to me in case she was restless in the night. He just said if she was restless to give it to her. He didn't say any time.'

[Gravely, and slow] 'She was quiet for about an hour? Then the spasms became much worse and you had to stay with her? You tried to get in touch with the Doctor by telephone but he was out?'

'I did not want to give her another injection.'

'Why not?'

'It was too soon after the previous.'

'But you did give that other injection?'

'I did. At 1 a.m.'

[Mournfully] 'What was the effect?'

'She became quieter and I called the other nurse because I could see that she was passing out.'

The Attorney-General: 'Did she pass out?'

'At about 2 a.m., as far as I can remember.'

It is time and the Judge stirs as if about to rise, people get to their feet but the movement is arrested by his voice and instantly the court freezes into immobility and silence. It is not the voice that had inquired about trays and bits of paper.

'You now understand', straight at Nurse Randall, 'that you must not discuss with anybody at all the evidence you have given or are going to give, and if you are wise you will avoid the company of the other nurses in this case so that there can be no grounds for complaint. Because if I do have any grounds for complaint I shall take a very serious view of it.'

And now the court is allowed to clear. We walk out trying to look unhurried, upright, and innocent.

DAY FOUR

COURT procedure has no regard for dramatic unity. This is the third consecutive morning on which we find facing us in the box a witness left over from the day before. We had thought that Sister Mason-Ellis's spell was long; little did we know what was in store. A whole full day with one witness on the stand, Nurse Randall and Nurse Randall alone, and Mr Lawrence not done with her when evening comes. It is a day of shuttling back and forth – not always chronologically – through the nursing books, the prosecution trying to throw doubt upon the identity of their unknown quantity, and Mr Lawrence trying to establish a nice normal medical atmosphere and to throw doubt upon a witness of the Crown. Mr Lawrence scores often, if bit by bit; and his bits are admirably put together.

A pleasure, undoubtedly, to lawyers (the well of the court is packed with watching barristers today); a pleasure also to the auxiliary professionals, the eighty crime reporters, novelists, and foreign correspondents supposed to be present. But what about the target of it all, the jury? Do the jury feel burdened and perplexed about the minutiae of this case, do they feel they are being led into the light or merely a dance around the mulberry bush? The jury, perforce, sit enduring, patient, mute. At times they appear to listen with intensity, at others to subside, and most of the time one cannot fathom anything about them at all.

The morning starts off with the Attorney-General winding up yesterday's examination-in-chief.

'Nurse Randall, when you recorded paraldehyde 5 c.c. as given by the Doctor on the night of Mrs Morell's death, how did you know it was paraldehyde?'

'I must have been told.'

'By whom?'

'By the Doctor.'

The Attorney-General lets this sink in. Then, 'Where did this paraldehyde come from?'

'I think the Doctor must have brought it.'

'Had you got any paraldehyde in that dining-room?'

'No, not then.'

Beginning on a new point. [Flatly] 'Where did you keep the nursing notebooks?'

Nurse Randall: 'In the drawer in the dining-room.'

'What usually happens to the books on the death of a patient?'

'I usually take them and keep them for a while and destroy them. We don't show them to the relatives. It's rather distressing for them.'

'Oh, quite.' [Getting warmer] 'What happened to *these* nursing books?'

But the answer is only, 'I don't know.'

[Circumambulating] 'The morning Mrs Morell died, did the Doctor arrive before you went off duty?'

'Well, I waited until 10 a.m. He did not arrive, and then I left.'

'Did the Doctor ever look at these books?'

'Sometimes, yes.'

The Attorney-General sits down.

It is not eleven, the day is before us. Mr Lawrence business-like begins at the beginning. Witness first went to nurse Mrs Morell in February 1949, was that so? Yes. 'She was not anything like a hale and hearty woman then?' She was an invalid. 'And she was an old woman?' She was. 'Rather a big woman?' Well made. 'You *were* aware that she was having regular morphia and heroin injections then?' She was only having morphia to begin with. 'Do you really think that – ? At any rate we have no records for that time. . . . She was certainly having morphia injections regularly?' Yes.

Mr Lawrence [gathering up the reins]: 'Frequently through-out the whole time she was showing restlessness? Especially at night?'

Nurse Randall: 'Yes, she was very restless.'

'You know that the object of the Doctor's treatment was to give her rest and sleep at night?'

[Dully] 'Yes.'

'That is quite true?'

'Yes.'

Apart, in the dock, the Doctor hears it all. His nurses on a case . . . memories of evenings when he came and went, on his round, coming in with his bag, stopping for a word, off again, a free man. . . .

'Can you say, as a nurse of experience, if that elderly lady with this brain trouble and so forth had been robbed of any sleep at night, it could have gone on long without trouble?'

'That's right.'

[Going forward, as it were, in steps of one syllable] 'And the treatment she was given was designed to secure the sleep and rest she needed?'

'Yes.'

'And I dare say you know this, don't you, that for months and months the regular treatment in the form of morphia and heroin injections hardly varied? Right up to about September 1950? It went without a change except occasionally when she had a brain-storm or disturbance of some sort and was given a little more to tide her over?'

'Yes.'

It is extraordinary how lulled the hearers are by Mr Lawrence's exposition. It has all become so simply sensible, such kindly common sense. One has to remind oneself that so far no one qualified has been asked whether this treatment was quite ordinary, or whether it was, as the prosecution has it, quite outrageous.

He now wants to deal, says Mr Lawrence, with the period in September when the Doctor was away in Scotland on a holiday and his partner Dr Harris was in charge. Look at what happened to the routine injection: ' "Morphia grains 1/4 *and* 1/8, heroin grains 1/3 *and* 1/6 given at 8 p.m. May have Omnopon 1/3 when necessary." We have not seen any reference to Omnopon before, now it appears here with Dr Harris. And it is also quite plain, isn't it, that on that night the usual injection was stepped up?'

Nurse Randall [neutral tone]: 'Yes.'

This is not quite enough to make the evening-paper men bolt for the telephone, but it makes everyone sit up.

Mr Lawrence [cashing in most smoothly]: 'Later that night

Dr Harris was telephoned for. Mrs Morell was wide awake, very restless and complaining of feeling queer. He came and – "Omnopon one tablet given. Two tablets to be repeated s.o.s." That was on Dr Harris's instruction?'

'Yes.'

'Omnopon contains 50 per cent morphia?'

'Yes.'

'You see the result of the treatment?' [Reading full tilt] ' "Seems very much brighter this a.m. and not so heavy. Has taken breakfast well. Disturbed by mice – " *Mice?*'

'Real mice.'

'Oh. Very unfortunate. Let us take stock of the position at this point. Obviously she was in a bad state of restlessness. Dr Harris had to deal with it because the Doctor was away, and he does so by increasing the morphia and heroin and introducing Omnopon at night?'

'Yes.'

'When later on her condition got worse that was exactly the way the Doctor tried to deal with it?'

'Yes.' There is just no other way for Nurse Randall to frame her answers. Here she is, a reluctant answering post.

Mr Lawrence: 'Everybody's endeavours were directed towards getting her some sleep?'

'Yes.'

'And from your notes it is quite clear, is it not, that *Dr Harris continued to use the same drugs the Doctor had been using?*'

'Yes.'

This is a good point. Mr Lawrence goes further. [Tone of bonhomie] 'It looks, doesn't it, as if the doctors, the Doctor and Dr Harris, coupled no doubt with good nursing, were coping with the case very well?'

He has been paving the way for the increases in drugs towards the end. As presented by him, it amounts to no more than this: Let them look at October, during those nights there has undoubtedly been an increase in the medication, has there not? But then they have the Doctor on the 31st ordering the omission of the morphia drugs and limiting it to one drug, heroin. That was an obvious change in the routine? And after a day or two of this limitation to heroin one finds improvement?

'Yes.'

Now come a sequence of brief projections. First the disposal of the suspicious point so often raised by the Crown.

'Mrs Morell was not very fond of the company of the nurses in her room?' No.

'It went to the length that the night nurse did not even sit with her at night?' Yes.

'They had to sit in the other room and only go in if she rang?'

Nurse Randall: 'Yes, and try to watch her.'

Mr Lawrence: 'And the way you managed that was to creep along and look in on her from time to time?'

'Yes.'

'And that was her wish?'

'Yes.'

And now the pay-off like a ready plum. 'And it was *her* wish that you were not in the room when the Doctor was there?'

'Yes.'

'When was it that anybody first asked you to try to remember tales about Mrs Morell's case?'

Nurse Randall: 'I think it was in August last year.'

'Who was it who asked you to remember about it?'

'Superintendent Hannam.'

'Did you make a statement then, a written statement?'

'Yes.'

But Mr Lawrence leaves it at that.

Mr Lawrence now has the transcript of yesterday's hearing in front of him. (The transcript is the typewritten copy of the shorthand notes taken by relays of shorthand-writers – twenty minutes to each bout – of every word spoken in the course of the proceedings. It is typed out every evening and becomes available to judge and barristers by about 9 p.m.) Mr Lawrence, his finger on the page: 'When my learned friend asked you if you had ever injected a mixture of morphia and heroin on the instructions of any doctor other than the accused, you answered, "No, I do not think I have." *Now* we *have* seen that you did that very thing on the instructions from Dr Harris?

'And the next question you were asked was whether you had ever given a routine injection of morphia and heroin on the instructions of any other doctor, and you said, "No," and that would not be quite right, and again for the same reason, would it not?'

Nurse Randall [resigned tone]: 'No.'

Not an entirely clean point.

By the end of the day, the listeners' very thoughts take shape in forensic pattern, answer or neat answer to a chainwork of hard-cast questions. The Judge winds up with one of his straight inquiries.

'What is the normal dose of paraldehyde, do you know?'

Nurse Randall: 'It depends how you give it, but I think 4 c.c. or 5 c.c. is a very large dose.'

The Judge: '2 c.c. would be the normal dose?'

'It would.'

'Is it a dangerous drug?'

'It helps to make you sleep.'

Mr Lawrence rises [to witness]: 'I must challenge what you said.' [Clearest note] 'Do you know what the British Pharmacopoeia dose is of paraldehyde? I must put it to you formally that the B.P. full dose is 120 minims or 8 c.c. Do you know that?'

Nurse Randall: 'I did not know that.'

Mr Lawrence [smooth as silk]: 'Of course not, you cannot be expected to know all these things.'

'And that ought to be that for Pelion on Ossa.'

'Shouldn't count on it; a fact in law has nine lives.'

DAY FIVE

NURSE RANDALL once more all morning, and Sister Bartlett, a young nurse, in the afternoon. The last working day of the first week. The cross-examination becomes a tug of war between defence and prosecution witness. The nurses, the defence suggests, brought a distorted tale to the investigators, and this is shown up by the entries and omissions in their own nursing records. One begins to realize how hard it is to establish a fact, any fact, unequivocally – there isn't much that could actually be proved beyond a reasonable doubt. Here, at the end, it will all go by impressions; the measure will be a more or less rationalized compost of emotion cum experience cum intuition. Truth, in a court of law, is circumscribed and its pursuit an elaborate rounding up and pinning down, until the dénouement when, almost quixotically, all is set loose again as the caged quarry is handed over to the jury with the explicit invitation to test and pluck the bars.

Mr Lawrence starts off with a little explanation. He hopes, he says, it is clear that s.o.s., a form of words frequently met in the nursing records, has nothing to do with the distress signal. S.o.s. – *si opus sit*, if need be. Next he asks the members of the jury and the witness to get out their books. Last volume; last night. Is he right, when he looks at his copy, in thinking that the report contains five separate entries for that night, one after the other, and each of them timed? He will read them.

' "10.30 p.m., paraldehyde 5 c.c. given by the Doctor."

' "11.30 p.m., very restless. No sleep."

' "12.30 a.m., restless and talkative and *very shaky*." Very shaky underlined twice.

" '12.45 a.m., seems a little quieter; appears asleep. Respiration 50."

' "2 a.m., passed away quietly." '

[With hard emphasis] 'There is no mention here on this

night from start to finish of any twitchings or jerkiness at all?'

Nurse Randall: 'No, not here.'

Mr Lawrence: 'I want to ask you about the evidence you gave to my learned friend, the Attorney-General, about this jerkiness.' [Very cold] 'May I ask you to look again at your record for two nights *before*. Do you see that under the entry for 4 a.m. you have written "Twitchings more pronounced"?'

'Yes.'

'That was the word you used – in the best way you could – to describe the condition?'

Nurse Randall: 'At that time.'

'What you told my learned friend was in substance this, that the words "very shaky" on the last night were meant to include the jerkings?'

[Woodenly] 'Yes.'

'Do you still say that?'

'Yes.'

[Pressing] 'After all the answers you gave the other day about how accurate you were in your notes and how important it was to be accurate?'

[Mumbling] 'This was written after the patient had died.'

Mr Lawrence [very much on top of it all; using a note of incredulity]: 'Are you standing there in the face of this record made by you on the patient's last night, are you standing there and saying as a trained nurse of twenty-five years or more experience that when you wrote these words "very shaky" and underlined them, they were intended to mean something quite different from what they had meant when you had used those very words in earlier reports?'

[Truculent] 'Yes, I do. They were more intense.'

[Lash] '*What* was more intense?'

[Muttering, low voice; but sticking to it] 'The shakiness and the jerkiness.'

Mr Lawrence [softly rational]: 'Why, if you were recording something quite different, did you use *the same words*?'

Nurse Randall: 'I just don't know. I suppose I wrote it down quickly.'

One would give a good deal by now to learn the whole truth.

Mr Lawrence: 'Let me suggest to you the reason why you used the same words. The reason was that you were describing the same shakiness that you had often described in the past months; it was greater in degree – that is why you underlined – but still the same kind.' [Flinging it at her] 'That's it, isn't it?'

Nurse Randall: 'I can only remember how very dreadful they were, the jerks.'

[Cold water] 'That is what you say now; but at the time you only put down "very shaky", didn't you?'

Now, one curious thing is that the significance of this jerkiness has still not been mentioned in the proceedings, so that the jury may well have no idea what it is all about. Shaky or jerky, *le mot juste*, it may all appear to be some habitual extravagance of the legal mind. There is no doctor on this jury (doctors are generally excused), and surely they do not do such things as ring up their medical friends in the evening. Or do they? No one knows what a jury does or thinks or talks about in the jury-room. Not that there appears to be anything as explicit as a law, a – British – jury is simply hedged with tacit taboos. They are asked no questions, and publish no answers. (Some thirty years ago a newspaper article did appear that was based on an interview with a juror; it was described by the then Lord Chief Justice as 'improper, deplorable, and dangerous'.)

Suddenly the Judge, who rarely intervenes while counsel is in possession, asks as if compelled, 'Have you got *now*, as apart from what was written down, a clear recollection in your mind of her being jerky an hour before she died?'

Nurse Randall, as if beside herself, 'I have! and I never want to see anything like it again.' It was a cry from the centre of some nerve, hysterical perhaps, but as though she had touched on something she had lived.

Some of the seats have emptied. People have crept out into the hall, to send off the latest or just to smoke, for air. . . . Looking back through the glass panels of the shut door, one can see into the court – wigged heads, writing hands, the Judge enthroned, red-robed, heraldic like a king of cards; the back of the Doctor's head and neck solid above the parapet; the small woman, face puckered, in the box; counsel in shadow-play shooting out an arm; lips moving soundless: all silent, sharp, like fish inside a bowl.

Mr Lawrence: 'It is quite obvious, is it not, that she was not in a coma?'

Nurse Randall [holding on to the bone]: 'She would be in a coma or heavy sleep for a time after the injections.'

Mr Lawrence: 'A heavy sleep and a coma are not the same, are they?'

[Toneless] 'No.'

[Swift cut] 'Nurse Randall, are you trying to be as accurate as you can be?'

'I am, sir.'

'If a patient is described as awake she is plainly not in a coma?'

[Dully] 'No.'

[Turning it on] '*If a patient is described as talkative* she is plainly not in a coma?'

Nurse Randall: 'She would be rambling or not knowing what she was talking about.'

'*Are* you listening to what I am putting to you or not?'

'I am, yes.' Her face remains inscrutable.

[Quite rough] 'You told the Attorney-General that she was in and out of a heavy coma, didn't you?'

'I don't remember.' This, considering the transcript, is not wise.

[Dryly] 'Well, you can take it from me that this is what you said. Do you want to withdraw that now?'

'I probably meant heavy sleep.' The impression is that she is not so much trying to recall what happened as wishing to clear her own evidence. It is not unnatural.

'Do you want to withdraw or alter those answers?'

'I must have meant heavy sleep . . . ' [Blurring it again] 'She wouldn't respond to light or have her mouth cleaned, whereas if she was not in a coma she would have sucked a swab.'

But Mr Lawrence has it at his fingertips. '*That* is exactly what you recorded her as having done on the last night but one. In your report you say she had sucked a swab on forceps. Just point out to me any entry of yours in the last three nights that indicates that this woman was in a coma.' [Tough] 'Can you do it?'

'No.'

The barb planted, one can all but see him turn his back and walk away without a glance.

'You have *one* record of paraldehyde 5 c.c. given by the Doctor, but there is *no* record anywhere of any subsequent injection?'

It *is* relentless, yet there is no sense of bullying. These clashes are too grave, too detached, and also too histrionic. At a capital trial the charge, as it is intermittently remembered, is so extreme that the man who stands for the man so charged is himself in an extraordinary position. A bully operates in a lesser context. Even at his most crushing moments Mr Lawrence is a professional executing a task. People in the witness-box, finding their rudimental and unguarded recollections submitted to a kind of public X-ray, at times muddle or slide beside the truth, their second thoughts are so unlike their first. Once on that course, sweet reason cannot touch them. As to the present combat it is not, for all Mr Lawrence's inquisitorial expertise, entirely uneven. Mute resistance can be a heavy weapon.

'This was the last night of her life, wasn't it, and if the second injection which is not recorded *was* given by you – '

'I did give it – '

[Shaved ice] 'Allow me to finish the question. *If* this second injection was given by you, it was the last injection before her death?'

'Yes.'

'And it was given by you on your own responsibility as a nurse, having failed, from your own evidence, to get in touch with the Doctor?'

'Yes.'

[Crescendo] 'And within an hour of being given that injection the patient was dead?'

'Passed away, yes.'

[With great seriousness] 'Miss Randall, it is just not conceivable, is it, that you would have left that injection out of the record if you *had* in fact given it?'

That leaves her in a cleft stick. She either doesn't see it, or does not care. [Quite mulish] 'I did give it.'

Mr Lawrence: 'You cannot have it both ways. If it was a matter of some importance it would have gone into the book?'

Nurse Randall: 'I might have left it out because it was the last one and I had other things to see to.'

Not implausible.

Mr Lawrence: 'You have no *recollection* seven years later why it was not in the book?'

'No, I haven't.'

'Your memory isn't very trustworthy.'

[Snap] 'It appears not to be.'

'And if your memory *is* right about that injection, there was a serious breach of duty that night?'

Inevitable assent.

'When did you leave the house on the morning after Mrs Morell's death?'

'At ten o'clock.'

'You did not wait for the Doctor? And your patient was dead?'

'Yes, passed away.'

'*And you did not wait?*'

'I was supposed to get off at nine.'

'You had been with her for nearly two years and you waited only one hour? When the Doctor was not there at ten o'clock you went?'

'What was it you did not want Sister Mason-Ellis to tell?'

'I don't recollect.' [Mr Lawrence is waiting] 'It could only be alluding to the key, once Sister had said the drugs were in a cupboard and I knew it was in a drawer and there was no key. We had no key.'

Mr Lawrence: 'Sister Mason-Ellis told us that when you and she and Nurse Stronach were discussing this case in the train, it was you who said to Sister Mason-Ellis who was then in the witness-box, "Don't say that or you will get me into trouble." '

Nurse Randall: 'I do not think she could have been meaning myself.'

'*Did* you say that?'

'I do not remember saying it.'

'Do you mean you don't remember something that happened Wednesday, two days ago?'

[Sticking to it] 'Yes.'

'Is that the sort of memory you have?'

'No. But if I did not say it' [pause] 'I would not remember it, would I?'

'Nurse Randall, are you being frank with me over this business in the train?'

'I am as far as I can be.' Always the unaltering face.

Mr Lawrence: 'Does that mean you are saying Sister Mason-Ellis was wrong?'

'It does.'

Mr Lawrence desists.

'When the Doctor went away on his holiday in September 1950, Mrs Morell was very much upset?' Yes, very. 'He came back all the way from Scotland for a day or two to see her? Did she tell you that she was going to alter her will and cut the Doctor out of it?'

'Yes, she did. She was very angry at the time.'

('Then she *must* have told the Doctor, too.' 'Why doesn't he say so?' '*He* will. It isn't his turn yet.')

Mr Lawrence: 'You, among a number of people, were a legatee under her will. How much did you get?'

Nurse Randall: 'Three hundred pounds.'

And that ends the cross-examination of Nurse Randall by counsel for the defence.

The Attorney-General takes an hour – chiefly with the nursing records – and nothing seems much shifted at the end of it. One answer is satisfactorily startling. 'Mrs Morell told me,' said Nurse Randall, 'that the Doctor had promised her he would not let her suffer at the end.'

The final stock shot is triple-barrelled, and the result is not quite what the prosecution may reasonably have expected.

'Apart from the Doctor, and possibly Dr Harris when the Doctor was away on holiday,' that much for the defence's casuistic point, 'have you ever had from any other doctor instructions to administer injections of morphia and heroin as a routine?'

Nurse Randall says that she cannot remember.

'Apart from the Doctor – *and* maybe Dr Harris – have you ever had from any other doctor instructions to administer heroin and morphia when *you* considered it necessary in your own judgement?'

[Quite smugly] 'Yes, I have.'

The Attorney-General [coming again; entirely unperturbed]: 'Have you ever had instructions from a doctor other than etc., etc., etc., to administer dangerous *drugs when the patient was not suffering pain*?'

'Yes, if they are very excitable, to keep them quiet.' Really, Nurse Randall is not predictable.

There comes one of the rare moments when the lid seems to fling open and one feels one has at last a glimpse of the workings of the wheels. The Judge says, 'Mr Attorney – '

The Attorney-General rises.

'Mr Attorney, we all now know a great deal more about the medication in this case than when you opened it. Are you going to invite the jury to say that these two, or one – whatever it was – injections in 5 c.c.s were given by the Doctor with the intention of causing the death of Mrs Morell?'

The Attorney-General [speaking fast, gulping his words]: 'I do submit that they were given deliberately and that they accelerated the death of the patient, but I will not elaborate, my Lord. I adhere to that and I have medical evidence which leads me to say that.'

The Judge: 'I am very much obliged. This is what I wanted to know.'

And the lid is back again.

He turns unhurriedly to Nurse Randall. 'I should like to make something clear – did you know that the last injection given was in fact paraldehyde merely because the Doctor told you so, or also because of its distinctive smell?'

Nurse Randall: 'I don't remember the smell of it.'

The Judge: 'You did write down paraldehyde in the book?'

'Yes.'

'Then this is right – you *know* that it has a distinctive smell, but you do not remember it having a distinctive smell at the time?'

'Yes . . . No.'

'Looking back now, supposing you had been told it was paraldehyde, do you think you would have noticed the absence of smell, or not?'

'I suppose that in a syringe it would not smell so strong as when given by mouth.'

The Judge: 'That is what I had in mind. If it is in a syringe would any smell escape?'

'I should think that the syringe would smell of it.'

'At any rate, it is quite clear that at the time you made your entry there was nothing in your mind to suggest to you it was not paraldehyde?'

'No.'

And he goes boldly on to the question counsel did not ask, 'Had you ever got it in your mind that it was something else? Morphia or heroin in a 5-c.c. syringe?'

'No.'

Mr Lawrence, seemingly oblivious of this windfall, asks if he may put a further question to the witness. 'My Lord, did she know in 1950 that paraldehyde has this unmistakable smell?'

Nurse Randall says she did, and that really nails the point. The Judge rises. The court is adjourned for luncheon. Nurse Randall, after eight hours in the box, steps down.

On our return there is a fresh face. The ninth prosecution witness is a young girl. Her head is crammed into a grass-green knitted ski-ing cap; her skin is bright and smooth. She came upon the scene, we hear, three months before the death and stayed until the end.

'As a day nurse, *yes*.' [Slightly breathless, willing.]

Q.C. for the Crown is taking her over the whole ground. In her first report there is a reference to a special injection given by the Doctor, and two or three days after her arrival when she saw him give an injection she asked him what it was.

Sister Bartlett: 'He said it was a pick-me-up.' The voice is young and high.

Is it usual or unusual for a doctor to tell a nurse what he is injecting into the patient?

'Usual.'

While she was there did she notice any signs of severe pain?

She did not.

Did she ever apply her mind to the question of why Mrs Morell was drowsy all day?

[Brightly] 'She had had drugs all night. She slept on and off through most of the day.'

And what was her condition during the last few days?

'She was semi-comatose.'

Did Sister Bartlett notice anything in regard to Mrs Morell's movements that impressed itself on her memory?

She had twitching spasms. She remembered vividly the night before she died that they were very severe; it was mostly in the arms and legs. Yes, and she remembered the Doctor coming on the last night and giving her paraldehyde, and Mrs Morell went to sleep, and the Doctor came to the dining-room and prepared another syringe which he gave to Nurse Randall. She remembers that, but not what was in the syringe. She was in the room just before Mrs Morell died, she still had faint twitchings. Yes, and she was present when the Doctor arrived next morning. The nursing books? Wait a minute, yes, the last time she saw them was when the Doctor called that morning. He read through the report. No, she doesn't remember seeing them after that.

When it comes to Mr Lawrence, he has practically got to push her into saying she is glad the nursing records have been found.

'When did you first become aware they had survived?'

'When I read about it in the newspapers this week.'

Mr Lawrence: 'Are you, like Sister Mason-Ellis, glad to know that they survived?'

'I never really thought about it.' [Without self-consciousness] 'I don't think I quite understand.'

Mr Lawrence explains; she agrees; and once again out come the books. She has recorded no indication of twitchings or jerkings; she recorded, 'Awake, restless, talkative'?

Diffident mumble.

'Yes, Sister Bartlett – ?'

'... if I may take it off, to hear better?'

'Your hat?' [Kindly] 'You must ask his Lordship that.'

Turns speechless to the Judge.

He inclines his head.

Now they will turn to her next report. She came on at 4.45 p.m.? 'Has been very alert and talkative this evening. Morphia and heroin given with no effect.' [As if he had never read it before] '*No* effect? It had no sedative effect?'

Sister Bartlett, who has pulled off the green cap, 'It had no effect at all.'

Soon we are back to our old friend in sheep's clothing, 'Did you know that it is not an opium derivative but a very old-fashioned, well-established remedy for sleeplessness? In fact, paraldehyde is one of the safest soporifics there is?'

[Nodding sagely] 'Yes.'

And now they will turn to September . . . to August . . . to October . . . Mrs Morell was in a very bad temper . . . Sister Bartlett recorded a special injection . . . The surgical boots ordered by the Doctor had been fitted . . . Dexedrine tablets given . . . Milk-and-brandy taken . . . Mrs Morell would not allow the nurses in the room . . . A new tonic prescribed by the Doctor. . . .

The afternoon is advancing. A Friday afternoon. Sister Bartlett is the last of the nursing witnesses. A week is nearly gone. . . . One tries to lift one's head above the miscellaneous litter, 5 c.c.s and 120 minims, brainstorms and the sugar ration, talkative and comatose, grains 1/3 given at 2 p.m. and the small quantity of celery. Where does it stand? What has it been all about? When the defence sprang the nursing books, it did not only shake the prosecution's apple cart, it put the cart before the horse, and before it had got going. Their original intention cannot have been to linger five days over the nurses' evidence; the pattern of the Crown case seemed to have been outlined in the Attorney-General's opening speech: the nurses to give background evidence, preliminary sketches of sheer facts, to be followed, and followed soon, by expert interpretation. Instead, there came the nursing books which made it possible for the defence to dispute every single fact, and dispute it at great length; the experts were postponed and the case got stuck on the nurses' evidence, really like the needle on the gramophone. It is this which has infused the proceedings of the whole first week with a sense of unreality and method in a vacuum. The defence has been firing well and hard at a structure not yet properly set up, impossible to tell the damage or to decide if what has come down is the roof, the rafters, or a scaffolding.

Mr Lawrence, the indefatigable, the dutiful, is putting to Sister Bartlett, 'This policy of keeping her quiet was general among the nurses, was it not?'

'Oh, yes.'

[Brisk and kindly] 'That looks as if the utmost efforts were being made under the Doctor's orders to keep her as mobile and active as possible?'

Sister Bartlett [keen, open-mouthed, serious]: 'It *does*, yes.'

THE SECOND WEEK

THE DOCTORS

DAY SIX

Two days off go very quickly. On Monday morning everybody is back again like a well-rehearsed tableau vivant. One has a sense of not having been away at all, of having been here since the beginning of time.

'We're supposed to get cracking today.' There is always someone who has heard, goodness knows from where. 'Harley Street this afternoon. The prosecution wants to finish by Wednesday.'

'Yeah, and our boys will be home for Christmas.'

'Lawrence's going to call the Doctor and no one else.'

'He'll talk his head off!'

'Must be longing to; wouldn't you?'

'*Think* of a cross-examination, whatever you haven't done.'

'There's the other indictment. It's been kept very dark, the jury isn't supposed to know.'

'Are you *sure*?'

'Well . . .'

'You mean if he got off for this, he's going to be re-arrested? Just like that?'

'That's what I hear.'

The three knocks: the talk cut dead. The Judge's swift entrance; the bows; the rustle of settling down.

The Doctor has developed an affecting trick. Every morning as he is shot up through his trap-door – put up, they call it, 'Put up the prisoner', warders, watches in hand from cell to stairs, hiss at each other below-stage – the Doctor, too, bows to the Judge, a formal little bow, unacknowledged. And this he repeats four times a day, before and after every rising and adjournment, one professional man to another across the abyss.

Saturday and Sunday spent in prison in the middle of one's trial must be one of the great nervous ordeals.

The day turns out disorganized and patchy. Witnesses are

called and go on with the maximum lack of sequence. The jury does not grumble. It has been assumed for so long that they cannot show their feelings that they have ceased to do so. Victorian juries used to grow quite restive. We begin with last week's Sister Bartlett ready like a burnt offering in the box, a candid smile upon her face. An hour with the nursing books is endured by all. Then, the Crown deals the *coup de grâce* in a re-examination of four minutes. The box stands empty for a while. The clerk reads depositions from formal witnesses excused appearance. 'The undersigned, Harry G., of such and such, van driver, declares that he has made regular deliveries of parcels from Messrs Browne the chemists and handed them to various people at Mrs Morell's back-door.' So much for the drugs. 'Miss Ethel Julia Dockerell, of etc. etc., declares that she worked for Mrs Morell as a daily help, her duties including the cleaning of her bedroom. "I saw and talked with her every day. She did not at any time complain to me of severe pain." '

The chauffeur is called in person. A trim man; self-possessed. He tells about his mistress's illness.

'She was stricken while staying with her family in Cheshire, sir. . . . I used to lift her into her wheel-chair and push her about the garden . . . '

Counsel for the Crown: 'What kind of a car had Mrs Morell?'

Mr Price, the chauffeur: 'Rolls-Royce, sir.'

'What happened to this car after her death?'

'I took it to the Doctor myself, sir.'

'Did you see the Doctor?'

'Yes, sir.'

'What happened?'

'The Doctor came out and looked at it, and I left it there.'

Mr Lawrence, in cross-examination, 'A Rolls-Royce – what kind of a model?'

'1938, sir.'

'Mrs Morell was a generous woman?'

'Very generous to me, sir, and to other people as far as I am concerned.'

Mr Lawrence: 'After your three years' service as her chauffeur you benefited under her will?'

'Yes, sir.'

'How much did she leave you?'

'A thousand pounds, sir.'

Depositions from the funeral assistant who arranged Mrs Morell's cremation; from the removal foreman who went to fetch a large chest, 'I collected it and took it down to the Doctor's house.'

No other servants of Mrs Morell's are called.

The Attorney-General says he will now call Mr Sogno, solicitor. The usher comes back and reports that Mr Sogno is not present. The Attorney-General looks at his papers and says in that case he will call Detective-Inspector Pugh of the Eastbourne Police. Detective-Inspector Pugh, who has been in court every single one of these days, springs from his seat and is on his way to the box. Mr Lawrence rises and asks his Lordship whether he might say that the appearance of this witness in the box today is something of an embarrassment to him. He sounds reasonable and perplexed. He has been furnished, he says, through the kindness of the Crown with a list of witnesses and the order in which they propose to call them, and Inspector Pugh's name does not appear for some time. Indeed none of the police evidence appears until after the medical evidence. Moreover, Detective-Inspector Pugh is not the chief officer who dealt with this case. He wonders whether in the circumstances something else could not be done?

There cannot have been much rest over the week-end for the team of counsel.

The Attorney-General says he is sorry his learned friend is embarrassed. He does not wish to call the medical experts until after the recall of the chemist who gave evidence on Day One. There are certain calculations to be made and he is not ready to go back into the witness-box.

The Judge asks Mr Lawrence, 'Is it your difficulty that the police evidence has been called at all? Or is it that, if the police evidence is to be called today, this witness is not the principal witness?'

'My Lord, it is both. I had no reason to suppose that any police evidence was going to be reached at all today, and certainly not the second of the officers. This is my real difficulty. With the complexity of the medical position, I was under the impression that was going to be dealt with first.'

The Attorney-General says that perhaps it might help if the prosecution had no objection to his learned friend's reserving his cross-examination of Detective-Inspector Pugh. He adds that Mr Sogno might become available later on; Dr Harris, the Doctor's partner, was not available today.

One begins to see how tricky it is to keep the witnesses on a string during a long trial.

And so Detective-Inspector Pugh, who has been waiting on the steps like a dancer in the wings, streaks into the box. He is a lean man, wiry, with brown wavy hair and not a trace of nervousness in his smart bearing. He reels off the oath, straightens himself to face the Attorney-General, and shoots off from his notebook in a practised carrying voice, pat and rapid over fast familiar ground. 'On November 24th 1956, I went to the home of the accused at 8.30 p.m. with Detective-Superintendent Hannam and Detective-Sergeant Hewitt of Scotland Yard. Superintendent Hannam asked to go into the surgery and the accused said, "There is no question of a statement for I have been told not to make one." We went into the surgery, and there was some conversation between the accused and the superintendent. Then the superintendent said to him, "I have here a warrant directing Detective-Inspector Pugh to search the house under the Dangerous Drugs Act." ' Hint of courtesy pause.

The Attorney-General: 'What did the Doctor say when the warrant was read to him?' Parts are reversed now: long answers to brief questions.

Detective-Inspector Pugh: 'He said, "There are no dangerous drugs here. What do you mean by dangerous drugs?" The accused walked over to a built-in cupboard on the right-hand side of the fireplace. He opened one of the cabinets there and turned round to the superintendent and said, "I have quite a bit of barbiturates here" – '

Here, however, the flow is halted. Mr Lawrence, who must have been in ambush, puts in very hurriedly, 'My Lord, I must make a submission in the absence of the jury.'

The Judge looks at the Attorney-General –

There is the usual interchange, and at the end the Judge directs the jury to retire to their room. It is also considerately decided that they might as well begin to have their lunch. Public and press remain. Mr Lawrence submits that the next part of the detective-inspector's evidence is damaging to his client while irrelevant to the case, and should not be heard. The Attorney-General submits that it should. The Judge rules that it is admissible, and the court also rises.

The detective-inspector's disclosures are fated to remain suspended for a little longer. After the short adjournment, Mr Sogno appears to have become available – the Missing Witness as he was already called on many a placard – and the prosecution seems unwilling to lose hold of him.

The Attorney-General: 'My Lord, I am interposing now with Mr Sogno – ' Mr Sogno steps up, brief-case in hand. 'Is your name Hubert Sogno? . . . and are you a solicitor? . . . and have you been practising at Eastbourne since 1930?'

Mr Sogno says that it is, and he is, and he has.

[Full monotone] 'And did Mrs Morell become your client in 1948?'

'She did.'

'Did she make a number of wills?' The questions sound as if they were being fetched up in a bucket, slowly, slowly, from a deep well.

'She did.'

'In April 1949, did you have a telephone conversation with the Doctor?'

Mr Sogno opens his brief-case, takes out his papers and arranges them. 'I had.'

'Will you describe this conversation?'

Mr Sogno looks at an agenda, and begins. 'The Doctor said he was telephoning on behalf of Mrs Morell who was extremely anxious about the contents of her will and she desired to see me urgently that day.'

'Did you go to see her?'

'I did.'

'And was a further will made?'

'Eventually, it was.'

'Did that will leave anything to the Doctor?'

Mr Lawrence: 'My Lord, I object. I do not think, with respect, that the contents of the earlier wills can be evidence unless they are properly proved.'

The Attorney-General: 'Very well. I shall not ask about the contents of the earlier wills.'

(Impression on the jury?)

The Attorney-General: 'Did the Doctor call at your office at any subsequent time?'

Mr Sogno, head in papers, 'He called about a year later, in March 1950; he told me that Mrs Morell had promised him many months before that she wanted him to have her Rolls-Royce in her will and she had remembered that she had forgotten to do this. She said she now wanted to leave the car to him, and also a locked box at the bank which he said contained some articles of jewellery. The Doctor said that although Mrs Morell was very ill, her mind was perfectly clear and he had no doubt that she was in a fit condition to make a codicil. I reminded the Doctor of some gifts Mrs Morell had made by cheque some months ago and which she afterwards regretted, and I suggested the matter should wait until Mrs Morell's son came, who was expected at the end of the week, but the Doctor said that she was very uneasy and wished to get the matter off her mind.'

Behind his fine hand, the Judge delicately yawns.

Mr Sogno: 'I suggested that he might ease her mind by pretending to receive the box and then handing it back to the nurses in the other room. The Doctor said, No, Mrs Morell seriously wished him to enjoy her gift. He told me I should prepare a codicil and that it could be destroyed later if it did not meet the approval of Mrs Morell's son.' [For the first time with colour in his tone] 'I told him that was quite impossible.'

Mr Sogno went again to Mrs Morell and in due time a fresh will was drawn up.

The Attorney-General: 'And on August 24th there was yet another will?'

There was, and this proved to be the last will, and in it the Doctor was left the oak chest with silver and, if Mrs Morell's son predeceased her, the Rolls-Royce car.

The prosecution leaves it at that.

Mr Lawrence, in cross-examination [*parlante,* easy]: 'Mr Sogno, when the Doctor talked to you on Mrs Morell's behalf, had he made a point to you that he wanted, *as a doctor*, that you should go without delay and deal with the matter so that her mind was at rest?'

[Dryly] 'He certainly asked me to go and see her without delay; I am quite willing to assume that was his reason.'

Mr Lawrence: 'All in all she made six wills?'

[Turning papers] 'She did.'

'Were you sent for again by her?'

'I was.'

'This time the Doctor was away? On holiday in Scotland?'

'He was.'

'That was in September 1950. And she was very angry with him?'

'She instructed me to prepare a codicil to her last will, the effect of which was to cut the Doctor wholly from any benefit whatever.'

Mr Lawrence: 'And was this codicil legally executed?'

'It was.'

[Quickening] 'What happened to it?'

Mr Sogno produces an envelope and holds it up. 'The codicil I would say is all in small pieces. It was torn up by Mrs Morell.'

'Did her tearing it up put the Doctor back into the will?'

Mr Sogno: 'Oh no. Tearing up a document is not an effective way of reviving gifts. The codicil cutting him out was never validly revoked before her death.'

Mr Lawrence: 'Let us get this quite clear. Mrs Morell never executed any document giving back the bequests to the Doctor?'

'She did not.'

[Letting the full meaning of this sink in] 'So that when she died in November the Doctor was not in any way a beneficiary under her will?'

'That is correct.'

'For *anything at all*?'

'For nothing at all.'

Mr Lawrence: 'So in short it comes to this – when afterwards the Doctor did receive the chest of silver it was really only by favour of Mrs Morell's son, the residuary legatee?'

'He said by all means the Doctor should have the chest because it was his mother's wish.'

'So the Doctor did not get the chest of silver *under the will at all*? And if he got the Rolls-Royce, it was also not under the will?'

Mr Sogno assents.

'Mr Sogno, another matter. Is there a clause in her will that says "I desire my body to be cremated"?'

'Yes; in all the time I was dealing with her that has always been her wish.'

Pause; then, conversationally, 'What *was* the final net value of Mrs Morell's estate before deduction of duties?'

Mr Sogno [reading]: '157,000 pounds.'

'There were several legatees under her will? There was Nurse Randall, who got 300 pounds?'

'There was.'

'The gardener got 500 pounds and all the dahlias?'

'Yes.'

'The chauffeur got a thousand pounds. And there were six legacies to various charities ranging from a pound to a thousand pounds?'

'Yes.'

[Flung off lightly] 'What was the probate value of the chest of silver received by the Doctor?'

Mr Sogno: 'Two hundred and seventy-five pounds and five shillings.'

Counsel for the defence sits down, as well he might.

Detective-Inspector Pugh is called back and does not seem put off his stroke. 'The superintendent told the accused that it was a search for dangerous drugs, like morphine, heroin, and pethedine. The accused then said, "Oh, that group. I very seldom use them. There may be a little phial of tablets in my car, but not more." The other officers looked in the cupboard of the surgery. When I asked the accused if he had any more dangerous drugs, he said, "Only those in my bag, the black one over there. There might be a little in that bag but nowhere else." '

The Attorney-General: 'Did you, in the course of your duty, go a second time to the Doctor's house?'

'On December 19th I went with Detective-Superintendent

Hannam. The superintendent told the accused that he was going to charge him with murder. The accused said, "Murder? Can you prove it was murder?" The superintendent said, "You are now charged with murdering her." As we were leaving the house, the accused and his receptionist clasped hands. I heard him mumble something I failed to catch, but as he turned towards me I heard the words, "See you in heaven." '

The Attorney-General: 'Thank you.'

Mr Lawrence half rises to say that he is not prepared to cross-examine at present, and the inspector smartly steps down.

'Detective-Superintendent Hannam – '

The superintendent, who had left the court during the other officer's evidence, comes in again. His appearance is familiar from the newspapers. He strides into the box, chest out, chin in, as a tenor might go forward for his aria.

The oath rings out. ' . . . and nothing but the truth. In 1956 I was making inquiries into this case at Eastbourne and on the evening of October 1st I met the accused by chance as he was putting his car away in his garage . . . '

But hardly under way, there is once more a check.

Mr Lawrence asks whether he might make a submission in the absence of the jury. The jury retires. The Judge listens looking at the deposition in front of him. The submission is upheld, it is ruled that part of the superintendent's evidence is not admissible. The jury returns. It is twenty-five minutes later.

Underneath the urbane cadences, the scrupulous observance – My Lord, in fairness . . . if my learned friend so pleases – underneath the casual orderly patience, there is a sense of iron inescapability. *There is no way out.* The prisoner in the dock is committed to his deed, committed irrevocably to one course between two points: the wheels are moving, nothing – nothing on earth – can stop them, and the wheels are going one way only, towards a verdict. Men, always and everywhere, have escaped against all but inconceivable odds. From enemy territory, from concentration camps, from Siberia; from nightmare conditions, against nightmare threats, over nightmare distances, from captivities guarded unimaginably other than by two warders doodling and nodding on two chairs. Nobody held on a capital charge has ever escaped from an English prison and an English court between an indictment and the sentence.

The superintendent, who has been waiting almost to attention in the box with an expression as if butter would not melt in his cheek, is off again. 'In my conversation with the accused that evening, reference was made to the chest of silver.' [*Vivace*] 'The accused told me, "Mrs Morell was a very dear patient. She insisted a long time before she died that I should have it in her memory. I never wanted it. I am a bachelor and I never use it. I know she was going to leave it to me and her Rolls-Royce car. She told me she had left it to me in her will. Oh yes, and another cabinet." '

The Attorney-General: 'Did you say anything to him in relation to the cremation certificate?'

[Deadpan] 'I said, "You have said on it that you were not a beneficiary under her will." The accused replied, "Oh that was not done wickedly. God knows it was not." ' And there comes all the rest of it, the dear relatives, and liking cremations to go off smoothly, and how it was not done deceitfully, just as it had been quoted by the Attorney-General in his opening. And here again the 'God knows it was not' is spoken not as if it were a figure of speech but as if it meant what it said, that God had been taken into the Doctor's confidence. It is a feature of all trials that whole sentences – perhaps spoken once by a defendant – are turned up and repeated word by word over and over in varying emphases by everybody from the prosecutor to the judge in summing-up, and it has a most curious effect.

The Attorney-General [*basso profundo*]: 'And on a later date did you go to the Doctor's house on a search for dangerous drugs? And what happened there?'

Detective-superintendent [*veloce*]: 'The accused said, "What do you mean by dangerous drugs – poisons?" I replied, "Morphine, heroin, pethedine, and the like." And the accused said, "Oh, you'll find none here. I haven't any. I very very seldom use them. I have perhaps, I think, one little phial of tablets in my bag, but no more." I then told Detective-Inspector Pugh to go and check that the blinds were secure in the front of the house.'

And the implication of that is that the blinds had to be pulled because there was a crowd of reporters and photographers waiting outside the house. How did they happen to be there, at 8.30 on a November night? Who tipped them off?

During the debate on the police evidence, it was managed with great skill not to disclose a word of the disputed evidence itself. Judge and counsel simply had the text in front of them. But that same evidence was heard by Press and public at the magistrates hearing a few months before. Reports of it were published and were read by a good portion of the inhabited world, and are still there to be read. This is what appeared in *The Times* of that day.

[Superintendent Hannam had expressed anxiety about some of the gifts the Doctor had received in wills from his patients, to which the Doctor replied]: ' "A lot of those were instead of fees. I don't want money. What use is it to me. I paid £1,100 supertax last year." [Later on when the Superintendent was searching the surgery for drugs]: 'The Doctor flopped into a chair in front of the desk, held his head in both hands, and appeared to be crying. When the search began he went to the right-hand cupboard and said that there were a number of barbiturates, but no drugs. The cupboard was very untidy, with a number of bottles lying around, some on top of each other. There were several boxes of chocolates – one slab had stuck to the shelf – and there were pieces of butter, sugar, and margarine. ... While the witness [Superintendent Hannam] was examining the cupboard, the Doctor walked slowly across the room to an identical built-in cupboard on the left-hand side of the fireplace, opened the centre compartment, and put his hand inside, then he took out two objects which he put inside his left-hand jacket pocket. The witness asked the Doctor what he had taken from the cupboard, to which the Doctor answered that he had only opened the cupboard for him. The witness moved towards him and said quite sternly, "What was it, Doctor?" He then took from his pocket a small bottle containing hyperduric morphia and a carton containing an identical bottle. The witness told the Doctor not to do silly things like this, for they were against his own interest. The Doctor replied, "I know it was silly. I did not want you to find it in there." Asked, he said, "One of those I got for Mrs Soden who died at the Grand Hotel, and the other was for Mrs Sharp, who died before I used it." '

The 'silly things like that' were not left at that. They did the Doctor an unending deal of harm. Harm, when they were brought up before the magistrates; harm, when it was decided not to bring them out at the Old Bailey, because it added to that sense of there being more to everything. (And ultimately he was prosecuted for them on two counts, obstruction of the police and wilful attempt to conceal certain drugs.)

Detective-superintendent [in the box; full spate]: 'I then showed the accused a list of the prescriptions ordered by him for Mrs Morell. The accused raised his hands and stopped me saying, "Now all these I left prescriptions for, either at the chemist's or at the house. She had nurses day and night." I asked who administered the drugs, and the accused replied, "I did, nearly all. Perhaps the nurses gave some, but mostly me." I asked if any were left over when she died, and the accused answered, "No, none. All was given to the patient." I said, "Doctor, you prescribed for her 75 grains of heroin tablets before she died?" He said, "It was all used. I used it myself." '

Does a man accused of murder think of escape? Can he consider it? The prisoner escaping from a camp is not just getting away, he is going *to* something; he is escaping, essentially, in order to be again himself. For a prisoner at the bar there is no such return. Bound to his deed, or to the shadow of his deed, liberation can only be reached through absolution or expiation, acquittal or the serving of the sentence that may be put upon him. Is there not in each of us a corner that is ready to relinquish choice, might it not be that in his heart of hearts a man so placed is most at rest under that inevitability?

'I said, "Doctor, I have no medical training myself, but surely the quantity of dangerous drugs obtained for Mrs Morell during the last week of her life would be fatal? and is pain usual with cerebral vascular accident?" The accused replied, "There may have been a couple of these final tablets left over, but I cannot remember. If there were, I would take them and destroy them. I am not dishonest with drugs. Mrs Morell had all these because I gave the injections. Do you think it was too much?" I said, "This is not a matter for me, Doctor, I simply want to get at the truth." I asked if he had any records of what he prescribed, and if he had a patient's clinical card, and he answered that he did not keep any records. He only recorded visits, and perhaps not that for private patients.'

The Attorney-General: 'In the course of your search was any morphia discovered on the premises?'

Superintendent: 'There were two bottles of hyperduric morphia found in his pocket – '

[Sharply and quickly] 'I did not ask you that!'

'... and small quantities in his bag. When he left we went through the dining-room; the accused pointed to a chest and remarked, "That's the famous Morell piece". Inside the chest were eight drawers containing silver, most of it was still in tissue paper.'

DAY SEVEN

THE morning is spent over the rest of the police evidence. The Attorney-General has not finished with the superintendent.

'Did you see the Doctor again?'

'Two days after my search, I saw him at his own request at police headquarters.'

'What did the Doctor say to you?'

'He said, "You told Mr James, my solicitor, there might be other charges. I am worried. What are they?" '

'What did you reply?'

'I said, "Mrs Morell is certainly one." ' Now we have again, Easing the passing of a dying person isn't all that wicked . . . that cannot be murder . . . it is impossible to accuse a doctor. . . .

Then comes the day of the arrest. 'I went to the accused's home with Inspector Pugh and Detective-Sergeant Hewitt. I said, "Doctor, on November 13th 1950 a patient of yours, a Mrs Morell, died and you certified the cause of death to be cerebral thrombosis. I am going to arrest you and take you to the local police headquarters where you will be charged with the murder of Mrs Morell." He was cautioned and said, "Murder?" He paused for a few seconds and then repeated, "Murder? Can you prove it was murder?" '

The Attorney-General: 'Did he say anything else?'

'He said, "I did not think you could prove murder. She was dying in any event." Then he put on his overcoat and we all went to the police station.'

'As you were going through the hall, did you see the receptionist?' We did. 'Did any conversation take place?' It did. 'What did you hear?'

Detective-superintendent: 'The Doctor said, "I will see you in heaven." '

Hardly, one might think, the words of a guilty conscience.

Mr Lawrence starts in this way, 'Let me go back to the beginning. The first interview with the Doctor about which you spoke took place on October 1st.' [Whip fast] 'Was it in the street?'

Detective-superintendent [*cantabile*]: 'It was.'

[Cat-smooth] 'Outside his house?'

[*Idem*] 'At the back of his house.'

'By the garage?'

'Yes.'

'Was it in the morning or the evening?'

[Still casually, cheerfully] 'It was in the evening. I met him at 9 p.m. and left him at 9.45.'

[Raised eyebrow] 'In October – in the dark?'

[Singing tone] 'Yes – in the dark.'

[*Legato*] 'Do I understand it was what you call an unplanned, casual meeting?'

[Smile beneath the skin] 'Oh, yes.'

'That means to say that the meeting was not by any design on your part?'

[Manly toss] 'It does.'

'It was rather a remarkable coincidence for a chance meeting, was it not?'

[Off-hand] 'I don't think so.'

'There were quite a number of coincidences that fell together, weren't there?'

[Slightly weak bravado] 'What do you mean by coincidences?'

[Sharply] 'You don't mean that you didn't understand my question, do you, Superintendent?'

[Level voice, smooth. But the smile is somewhere] 'It is impossible to understand what the coincidences were unless you help me to help you.'

Mr Lawrence [quite hard]: 'I will certainly help you. I may interpret the phrase "unplanned casual meeting" that the meeting was entirely by chance?'

'You may.'

'It so happened that at the very moment when the Doctor was outside his garage putting away his car you happened to be in his road?'

'I was passing by.' The Doctor's house in fact, as many know, is in a fairly central part of the town, which is not large.

Mr Lawrence [icily]: 'The coincidence I am suggesting to you is not only that he was putting his car away at a time when you were in his road but at the very moment when you were actually outside his house?'

Detective-superintendent [lightly]: 'Yes – passing by.'

'Very well. Let me go on. During this chance meeting you talked to the Doctor about this chest of silver?'

The superintendent asks whether he might have Exhibit 33, the notes he had taken at the time.

The Judge: 'Have you any objection, Mr Lawrence?'

'No, I want to be quite fair. If the superintendent cannot answer my question without his notes, by all means let him have them.'

Detective-superintendent [rapping out]: 'That is quite improper. I want to be accurate.'

The Judge [cold and final]: 'Do not intervene please when counsel is addressing me.'

Mr Lawrence, to the superintendent, 'Was that observation addressed to me?'

'No. It was an answer, I thought, to something *you* were saying to me.' The superintendent's 'you' has a veiled contemptuous ring.

Mr Lawrence: 'To whom was it directed if not to me?' There is something rather beyond the punctilio of law-court ferocity in this exchange, a note more of the antagonism between two scrapping males.

The Judge: 'Mr Lawrence, I think I have dealt with it sufficiently.'

Mr Lawrence [recovering instantly]: 'Let me put something quite squarely to you, Superintendent. This chest of silver was in the will, but at the time Mrs Morell died the Doctor had been cut out of the will altogether?'

'Yes.'

[Stressing] 'Did you know then, as you know now, that the only reason why the Doctor got the chest of silver was by favour of Mrs Morell's son?'

[Casually] 'Yes, I think I did.'

'Did you know at that time, too, that the Rolls-Royce was given to the Doctor by Mrs Morell's son?'

'I think so.'

[Energetically] 'Did you know – and do you know now? – that as to the other cabinet or box he has never had it at all from anybody?'

[Slack tone] 'I do know.'

[Sustained] 'You were drawing his attention to the cremation certificate at that time as if he not only were a beneficiary under the will, but *knew* he was a beneficiary under the will and had told lies about it?'

[Shrug] 'Yes.'

'And all the time *you knew* that he was not a beneficiary under the will?'

'The Doctor had said – '

'*You* knew, that is right?'

'The Doctor told me – '

'*Please* answer my questions.' [*Forte*] 'When you were asking him at your "chance meeting" about the cremation certificate *you knew in fact* that he was not a beneficiary under the will?'

Detective-superintendent: 'He had just told me *he* knew he was in the will.'

Mr Lawrence: 'If you were interested in finding out his state of mind or the condition of his knowledge in relation to the certificate, you could have asked him whether he knew in fact he was not a beneficiary under her will?'

[Scornful] '*His* state of mind – ? Of course I could have done.'

Mr Lawrence: 'That would have been a question the answer to which would have been very helpful at this stage.'

[Airy] 'I don't know.'

[Very serious] 'You could have asked this very helpful question, could you not?'

[Evidently hedging] 'This was not an interrogation, it was in the course of a very long statement.'

Mr Lawrence: 'I must put this to you: These matters that I just raised are not things that the Doctor said at all.' [Crescendo] 'They are reflections of things that *you were* saying and putting to him and to which *he* was making *no reply*?'

[Hackles rising] '*That is quite untrue*. These were his very words and I recorded them accurately.'

[Deflating] 'Well, this will be a matter for the jury to judge.'

[Switch] 'Let me come to November 24th. That was the occasion when you three police officers, Pugh, Hewitt, and yourself' [it sounds no more gracious than the superintendent's 'you'] 'went to the house at half past eight in the evening.' [Square look] 'What were *you* doing at all that night and by what authority?'

Detective-superintendent [if stung, it does not show; quite smoothly]: 'I was supervising and assisting in the search that Mr Pugh was making under the Dangerous Drugs Act warrant.'

Mr Lawrence: 'What police officer was authorized by this warrant to go to the house and conduct the search?'

'Detective-Inspector Pugh.'

'If you were supervising Pugh, what was Hewitt doing?'

[Lofty] 'He was assisting.'

[Stage surprise] 'Did you think that Detective-Inspector Pugh, the senior C.I.D. officer of the local police, was not competent or capable of executing that warrant?'

The Judge: 'I think you are right, this witness was a trespasser, but does that matter in this case if he was?'

There is a feeling that it does. The means making good the ends. At the back there is an exchange of looks. The degree of scrupulosity in the conduct of an investigation must be a pointer to the validity of the results obtained.

Mr Lawrence: 'I am coming to that. You police officers did not wait in the execution of your search or anything until Mr James, the Doctor's solicitor, arrived?'

[Again, the well-veiled smile] 'No.'

'What the Doctor did was to go into the surgery at once and try to ring up Mr James?'

[Putting this right] 'He asked me if he might do so and I gave him permission.'

'*You*, a trespasser in his house, giving him permission to ring up his own solicitor?'

The Judge: 'He has not admitted he was a trespasser. I said you were right he was likely to be a trespasser.'

Mr Lawrence [to the superintendent]: 'It amounts to this – you, not being named in the warrant, have just told me that you permitted the Doctor to ring up his solicitor?'

[Coolly] 'He asked my permission and I gave it.'

'Very kind of you. And then you sent Inspector Pugh out of the room instructing him to check whether the blinds were down in the front of the house. That left you and your assistant from Scotland Yard alone with the Doctor?'

'It did.'

'Neither of you being authorized to search?'

[Lofty] 'Under the warrant, no.'

Mr Lawrence: 'And then in the absence of the local inspector, there was all that conversation you said you had with the Doctor about Mrs Morell and the prescriptions and the amount of drugs she had had?'

'Yes, there was.'

'Inspector Pugh stayed out of the room for about twenty minutes and it was all finished when he came back?'

'That particular conversation was.'

Mr Lawrence: 'I suggest to you that when you said, "This is the list of the drugs prescribed for Mrs Morell," or words to that effect, the Doctor was across the room and just said quite casually, "Oh, yes?" '

[Rearing] 'Oh no, he was not! He was standing right beside me when I had that list in front of me.'

'And when you said, "Were they all given to her?", he said, "I cannot remember about that." '

[Throwing it off] 'No. Quite untrue. He was most emphatic about it.'

Mr Lawrence [as if he knew what he was talking about]: 'And when you referred in some way to the quantities prescribed, the Doctor refused to discuss the matter any further with you.'

Detective-superintendent: 'That is quite untrue. The whole thing. He was most loquacious, and always has been since I've known him.'

'I suggest that when you said something about drugs that were left over, he did not reply even to that.'

[Lurking derision] 'Oh, yes, he did.'

'And I suggest that he did not say he was not dishonest with drugs.'

[Warmly] 'Quite untrue.'

All at once Mr Lawrence turns it off and the superintendent follows suit. In court the weather clouds and clears as suddenly as it does on board ship in mid-Atlantic. The next phase is relaxed, two men engaged in straightening out something together. The superintendent says that this was an extremely involved investigation covering an enormous field, and it is often impossible for him to recall a particular detail. Mr Lawrence asks whether he could tell him something about the inflection of the Doctor's voice when he said murder, pause, murder, can you prove it was murder. Was it interrogatory?

Detective-superintendent: 'I think it is only fair to say this, that the Doctor was a very shaken man indeed. I am not prepared to say whether there was any inflection. He was very distressed.'

Mr Lawrence: 'I think we can leave it at that – very shaken. It was quite obvious that your announcement of his arrest for murder was a shock? I am asking you this in the absence of any recollection of the Doctor's of having said anything. I must rely on you.'

'I want to help you all I can. It certainly was a shock to him.'

'Now about these words, See you in heaven. I am bound to put it to you quite bluntly that the Doctor never said them or anything like it.'

'They were his very words.'

'We are agreed that Miss Lawrence, the receptionist, took hold of the Doctor's hand?'

'Yes.'

'Did he ask her for his warm overcoat?'

'Yes, she went upstairs for it.'

'Did he then ask her to fetch him something to read, and she went upstairs again and fetched him some books?'

'She did.'

'I am going to suggest to you that he never said these words.'

Detective-superintendent: 'They were very staggering words to me. I recall them quite plainly.'

'To whom were they addressed? Not to you police officers?'

[Dryly] 'I should not think so for a moment. They were addressed to Miss Lawrence, and if she has not heard them it was because she was turned away from him and he was talking very quietly and she was crying and was herself very distressed. . . . I would say I heard those words, sir.'

And this ends the cross-examination of the superintendent.

Inspector Pugh is now recalled for his postponed questioning by Mr Lawrence. Unexpectedly, Mr Lawrence is brief and mild. He only goes for two points. Did the inspector have any idea that he was going to be sent out of the room during the search? The inspector says he definitely did not. What was his impression of the Doctor when he was about to be arrested? He was stunned.

Detective-Sergeant Hewitt of Scotland Yard, after him, does not fare so well. He positively sings his oath before his evidence-in-chief and all but overtakes his prompter. It is the same story once again – the evening visit by the three police officers, and what the accused said when Inspector Pugh was out of the surgery, about Mrs Morell and the drugs and 'I did, nearly all' and 'perhaps one little tablet left' and 'do you think it was too much?' It all sounds identical; and for good reason.

Mr Lawrence's turn. [Gliding start] 'While you were telling my learned friend about the prescriptions and all the rest of it, when you were giving that evidence, you were refreshing your memory all the time from your notebook?'

There is indeed an open notebook on the witness-box.

Detective-sergeant: 'Not my notebook. The superintendent's. I didn't write any notes about the conversation.'

Mr Lawrence, leaning forward, '*Am I really hearing what you are saying?*'

'Yes, you are.'

[Shredded with incredulity] 'Has the whole of your evidence as to what the Doctor said been given from some notes which were made by another officer?'

[Subdued happy gasps in court.]

'Not the whole of it, not so far as the arrest is concerned, but the rest of it.'

Mr Lawrence [*vibrato*]: 'The vital part – the *vital part* of what was said in the surgery when Pugh was away on something and you and Hannam were alone – that part has been given by your refreshing your memory entirely from Hannam's notes?'

Detective-sergeant [deadpan]: 'Yes.'

'*Is it really true* that all the time you were giving your evidence, another man's notes were open in front of you in that witness-box?'

'I was reading them.'

Mr Lawrence: 'That accounts for the fact that what you said was word for word the same?'

'I should hope it would be.'

'Otherwise you were *mis-reading*?'

'Yes.'

The Judge: 'Did you take any *part* in the preparation of these notes?' This sensible question rather takes the head off the sensation.

Detective-sergeant: 'Mr Hannam said if I disagreed with anything I should tell him.'

Mr Lawrence [quick to respond to a changed angle]: 'Do you call that an independent record?'

'Yes. Because if there was something I had not heard I would not agree to it.'

'So really, to be quite fair and accurate, there is a composite record made by two officers in that one notebook?'

'That is quite right.'

Mr Lawrence [with energy]: 'I must challenge the whole of this record of this interview in the surgery, and it is my duty to put to you what *did* happen after the inspector had gone out. Did you know that Hannam was going to refer to Mrs Morell?'

'No. I was simply there to assist the superintendent.'

Mr Lawrence once more suggests with a great deal of assurance that the Doctor never said any of the things he is recorded as having said by the police.

Detective-sergeant: 'I remember quite clearly that he said, "They were all given".'

Mr Lawrence puts it to him that the Doctor never said anything beyond, 'It is no good, I cannot remember the details, and I am not going to discuss it.'

'This was not so – it was nothing like it at all.'

Mr Lawrence [flinging at him]: 'Where did you and the superintendent put all this down?'

'It was made in Mr Hannam's bedroom at the New Inn.'

'Is it the usual procedure for two police officers to get together and make one record, or for each officer to make his own?'

'I have done both on a number of occasions.'

Suddenly it is over. The Attorney-General rises to ask one

question in re-examination: had the detective-sergeant *signed* the record in the superintendent's notebook? He had.

And here we seem to be exactly where we were before.

It is not far from one, and the court is beginning to watch the clock, when who should walk into the box again but Nurse Randall. It is explained that on returning home after finishing her evidence last Friday, she recalled something and telephoned the police.

The Attorney-General [in his neutral tone]: 'What was it you recollected?'

Her audience is ready for anything.

'I recollected', she mumbles, 'that it is the usual thing to ring up the doctor in the morning and tell him the patient has passed away and what you have given last. The Doctor had been late that night and I didn't ring him till the morning, about six or eight o'clock. I told him that Mrs Morell had passed away and the injection was given.'

'Which injection?'

'The last injection I gave.'

'The 5 c.c. paraldehyde?'

'Yes.'

This reappearance gives the defence the right to another go. Can Nurse Randall have forgotten Mr Lawrence?

Mr Lawrence [tone of profound doubt]: 'When did you recollect this?'

'On Friday night.'

'You recollected it is the usual thing to do to ring up the doctor in the morning and tell him of the patient's death?'

'Yes.'

[Silky] 'You did not remember this at the time?'

'No.'

'You remembered you were the chief nurse and you were the person who would normally do that?'

'Yes.'

'It is quite *another thing* – is it not – suddenly to remember you not only told the Doctor Mrs Morell had died but that you had given an additional injection?'

[Mulish – unshaken] 'I gave the last injection.'

'Why did you tell him on the telephone that it was given?'

'I can't remember.'

'Although there is an hourly sequence of entries in your book for that night, as we have seen before, there is no mention in them of this injection?'

'Because I had rung the Doctor and told him.'

'To excuse yourself, you say there was no need to put the second injection in the book because you had already told the Doctor that Mrs Morell had died and there was, therefore, no need to put *that* in the book. But you *did* put it in the book?'

'Yes.'

And so ends Nurse Randall's second entrance. *Cui bono?*

Paraldehyde crops up once more after the short adjournment. The Crown's chemist, the one who was engaged in calculations, has appeared and he tells the court of an experiment he has carried out with a 5 c.c. syringe filled with that household remedy: he had left the syringe for an hour on a tray covered with a towel and all the time there had been about the room the unmistakable smell of paraldehyde. The crux of his evidence, however, is his summaries of the prescriptions and injections; and there is one summary which shows up the daily difference between the amounts of drugs recorded in the nursing books as injected, and the amount of drugs prescribed. According to this summary there were 30 more grains of morphia and 22 more grains of heroin prescribed than given during the last five days. This tabulates the discrepancy which has been on everybody's mind; now we know that it is some 50 unaccounted grains of opiates, which seems a vague good deal. It seems like an answer to a prayer that the very next witness is the first doctor called. He is not, though, as it turns out, one of the expert witnesses, volunteers paid a daily fee whose function it will be to analyse the facts, but a witness who is here because he must. It is the Doctor's partner.

Dr R. V. Harris is a professional man of young middle-age, quite buttoned-up, most likely for the occasion. Mr Melford Stevenson, Q.C., is examining for the Crown. There follows the usual swift routine extraction of background facts. Dr Harris has been in general practice since 1937; he was a member of a partnership with the Doctor and two other men; he made a few visits to

Mrs Morell in the Doctor's absence; he remembers her as an old lady who had had paralysis on one side and who was subject to cerebral irritation.

'Did you keep a record of the visits you made to her?'

'I did.'

No question is asked as to the number of visits. Q.C.: 'When the Doctor went away, did he leave any instructions?'

'He usually instructed other doctors to carry on with whatever treatment he had been giving.' Most witnesses thaw after their first few minutes, Dr Harris remains stiff.

'Did you *comply* with that instruction?'

'To the best of my memory, yes.'

So the Doctor's medication cannot have been so hair-raising.

'Was Mrs Morell angry and annoyed with the Doctor for having gone away on holiday?'

'To the best of my recollection, she was.'

Q.C. [bringing out the nursing books; Dr Harris is provided with a copy]: 'Can you tell the court why you gave that instruction increasing the morphia and heroin, and saying she might have Omnopon if necessary?'

'To the best of my memory,' the answers sound as colourless as one can make them, 'she was in an extremely irritable state over the fact that the Doctor had gone away and I must have increased the sedatives she was already having because of the cerebral irritation.'

This is accepted for the present. The examination goes on in a bland probing way for some little time, and comes to an end with the prosecution's stock question framed to a T. 'Dr Harris, have you ever in the course of your own personal professional practice prescribed morphia and heroin together for a patient suffering from cerebral thrombosis?'

[Hesitating] 'To the best of my knowledge, I have prescribed morphia over short periods of time.'

'Have you ever prescribed morphia *and* heroin as a matter of routine?'

[Qualifying tone] 'I cannot remember having to do that for any of my own patients.'

The cross-examination is expected with considerable alertness. But it is late. One of the many things counsel has to bear in mind is the slice of time in front of him. Mr Lawrence begins with great politeness, as one professional man considerately to another. (It must be extremely distasteful to a man like Dr Harris to go through any of this at all.) First of all Mr Lawrence establishes that Dr Harris has paid twenty-eight visits to Mrs Morell, seven in May, one in June, and twenty in September. One realizes that the prosecution has kept the number vague, because there is something for the jury to reflect on in the very fact that a respectable doctor, even if a partner, has had real contact with the patient without becoming suspicious or raising an alarm. *Not* just a few visits? says Mr Lawrence. The poor old lady was subject to attacks of restlessness? Irritability? Sometimes even irrationality? Dr Harris can but agree. This was exhausting for her, was it not? and might lead to further trouble and even to another stroke? Yes. And that might be fatal? Dr Harris is led along. So the object of a treatment for a woman in those circumstances must be to avoid as far as reasonably possible these attacks of cerebral irritation? Dr Harris says, yes.

Mr Lawrence: 'And the way to do that, is to use what is called sedation?'

'Well, yes, I think a general practitioner would choose, to the best of his ability, a suitable medication for the effect he wanted.'

Dr Harris is not an overflowing witness.

Mr Lawrence continues to call his spades a spade. 'There is no doubt, is there, that the Doctor was using the morphia and heroin to give this patient the sedation which was necessary?'

'It was the line of treatment that he thought necessary.'

[Always in the tone of reasonable inquiry] 'When you yourself increased the amount of morphia and heroin – as you did on September 12th, did you not – that was the proper line of medical treatment that *you* thought necessary?'

'I agree.'

'Dr Harris, when you took over the case from your partner – two months before her death, wasn't it – you were confronted with signs of the patient's deterioration?'

'Yes, I believe her condition was showing that.'

'And this, too, is clear – that you *knew*, having attended her already in May and June of that year, that she was on a regular course of sedation by daily injections of a compound of morphia and heroin?'

Dr Harris: 'I knew she had been put on that line of treatment.'

[Still conversational, at the same time bringing out his point] 'Is it a fair summary to say that when you were in charge you continued the same type of treatment *and increased* the morphia content in the form of Omnopon?'

[Blankly] 'Yes, I was asked to continue the same treatment and I increased the same drugs that were being used.'

'Dr Harris, in the questions I am asking you there is no intention of criticizing you in any respect. The treatment as we have seen gave some good results and some not so good?'

'There was some temporary benefit at the time.'

Mr Lawrence: 'When you looked after her in September she had survived her stroke for two years and four months?'

Dr Harris: 'To the best of my belief, she had.'

[Urbanely] 'Not bad, was it? Not so bad for the Doctor's treatment?'

[Slowly, but warming to it] '*No* . . .'

'Is it often that women of that age survive a stroke as long as that?'

Dr Harris: 'It is very rare.'

(The Doctor's words, 'She was dying anyway.')

Mr Lawrence: 'And the treatment – under which she survived for two and a half years – was not a question of avoiding pain, it was a question of avoiding outbursts of irritation which might exhaust her?'

Dr Harris, who tries to be as honest as he can and who also has begun to blossom under Mr Lawrence, says very slowly with a smile that transforms him, 'I have a vague idea that she did suffer a certain amount of pain.'

DAY EIGHT

'It's a cinch.'

'A walkover.'

'With Dr Harris it's become so *improbable.*'

'One doesn't see how he wouldn't have smelt a rat or said so – if rat there was.'

'The vanishing rat.'

'He may have kept his eyes shut.'

'Cold fish, Dr H. Cagey.'

'Cagey respectable. Not cagey fishy.'

'Beats me why the prosecution called him at all?'

'The way I figure it, Dr Harris either belongs with the defence or in the dock.'

'There isn't supposed to have been anything wrong yet, at the time he was around. . . .'

'You can't split it up that way; it *all* hangs together or it just doesn't.'

'Well it doesn't.'

'*So far.*'

'Oh, we've heard all there is to it.'

'Judge's going to throw out the case. You wait – he's got to.'

'I *guess* the defence is home.'

'It's in the bag all right.'

'A walkover.'

This is the day on which the French and American press carry a story of the Doctor's having ordered himself a new motor-car. Later in the morning, Dr Douthwaite, principal expert witness of the Crown, makes his first appearance.

Dr Harris has a fairly light morning. Medical shop – *how* Mr Lawrence has managed to pick it up – all to a purpose. Respiration: a high rate has been recorded in the books – now is it not precisely an effect of drugging to *lower* the rate of respiration? Yes, says Dr Harris, but qualifies it by speaking of pulmonary congestion. Twitchings: there is a record of twitchings in her *left* arm; we know it was her left side that was paralysed – is it not usual in these cases to find twitchings on the bad side? It is not uncommon, says Dr Harris.

At the prosecution's end of counsel's row someone is seen making a note.

Mr Lawrence: 'The ordinary general practitioner would interpret that twitching as an indication of the brain damage caused by cerebral thrombosis?'

'It could be that.'

Mr Lawrence wants it neater. 'It would be a *reasonable* conclusion?'

Dr Harris: 'Yes.'

Re-examination snipes chiefly at the witness's credibility. The prosecution tries to show that Dr Harris did not tell the truth about the number of times he saw Mrs Morell. Five of the visits he referred to are not found entered in the nursing books. The Crown is using the original defence argument – no nursing-book entry, no doctor's visit.

This uncertainty about the visits is one of the small loose ends that is not cleared up. Faulty memory on Dr Harris's part? Hardly, as he read from his own contemporary records. A deliberate untruth is even more unlikely, as surely he could have no wish to increase his connexion with the case. Were the nursing books then after all not entirely reliable? Records, too, have their origin by human agency; to put absolute trust in them, may well be another modern form of hubris. One is left with a sinking sense of the general hopelessness of rediscovering the past, the whole past, *the way it was*. But the ends of a court of law are relative, limited, and temporal; the best must be made, here and now, of the best that can be got – fallibility is not a spectre but a calculable risk, and we plod on.

Q.C. Parting question: 'Dr Harris, have you ever *seen* the kind of twitches or jerks that result from heroin or morphia intoxication?'

Dr Harris: 'I cannot honestly say that I have.'

'Doctor, you were asked yesterday about the choice of drugs in a case of this type, and you said, I think, that it rested with the doctor in charge to select the drugs to produce the best results?' The Judge has made his half-turn to the witness-box. There is a pleasureable sense of rational anticipation.

Dr Harris: 'Yes, it would be up to the doctor to use what he considered best for the patient.'

The Judge [very light on the reins]: 'What sort of drugs have you got in mind, Doctor, from which a selection could be made?'

'In answering that question you must remember that this was 1950 and that there are more recent drugs which are used now. Then, there was phenobarbitone, bromides, and sometimes paraldehyde. That is the main group of drugs which could be used.'

'What about morphia and heroin?'

Dr Harris: 'I can only speak from my own experience that I have had to use morphia in this type of case over a short period of time.'

'A doctor who was selecting drugs for this type of case would be likely to select them from the barbiturates?'

Dr Harris [mind on the subject]: 'I should imagine that would probably be a first choice, except if the patient had acute cerebral irritation, and then he might have to use stronger drugs to cover that period.'

(If opiates are in fact given for irritation as well as pain, why had the prosecution so far professed complete ignorance of this?)

The Judge: 'By stronger drugs you mean – ?'

'Preferably morphia.'

'Heroin is a stronger drug than even morphia?'

'Yes; I have not used it myself very much, so I can't speak from great experience.'

The Judge: 'In considering your choice of drugs and in particular considering whether or not to use morphia or heroin, would you have regard at all as to what the after-effects might be, the long-term effects of the drug?'

Dr Harris [quite at ease now; almost with animation]: 'One *would* have to consider the long-term effects, but it is not always easy to know how long that length of time is going to be.'

Throughout this duologue the jury sits tense, lively attention on their faces.

'It has been suggested that because of the after-effects of morphia and heroin they ought only to be used in cases of severe pain?'

Dr Harris: 'That is the usual indication for the use of these drugs.'

'Medically speaking, would it be right or wrong to use morphia or heroin where there is no severe pain?'

'One might have to use them, particularly morphia, in the case of acute restlessness. Again I am speaking of 1950.'

'Doctor, I want to ask you some questions on another topic – about carrying out the treatment of another doctor. You said, I think, you followed the instructions you were given and you don't, I understand, make a new diagnosis of your own and prescribe new treatment?'

'No. In a case where one is only going to see the patient for a few days one would not change the treatment that had been instructed.'

The Judge: 'Now *how far* does that go? Supposing you were called in, as you were, to deputize for another doctor and you came to the conclusion that the treatment being given was harmful to the patient and would undoubtedly shorten life, would you say nothing about it at all and just carry on?'

[Pause] 'My Lord, that is a very difficult question to answer.'

'Would you carry on without saying anything? in this case to the Doctor?'

[Pause] 'The Doctor had definite ideas of treatment which were not necessarily my own, and I do not think I would have been in a position to have said anything to him.'

The Judge: 'But supposing you thought – rightly or wrongly – that the treatment was harmful and might shorten life?'

Dr Harris: 'Well, if I may speak in respect to this patient, it would have been in my opinion very wrong for me to have suddenly started to withdraw morphia and heroin from her for a few days. It might have made her extremely ill.'

The Judge: 'Yes, yes.' [Trying again] 'But *supposing* you came to the conclusion – leaving aside for the moment what steps you would take – that the treatment was harmful and likely to shorten her life, would you have done something about it or would you have just said, that is not my affair, I will carry on?'

There must be an answer to this. But no:

'I think if one is seeing a patient just for a few days and at the time one feels it is not doing the patient harm over that short period of time, one would not change the treatment.'

The Judge: 'Do you recollect ever *discussing* with the Doctor whether it was right or wise for her?'

Dr Harris: 'I cannot remember discussing it.'

He does not say – I did *not* think the treatment wrong or unwise. He does not say – Yes, my Lord, it does go as far as this: it is not one's affair, one just carries on. Nor did he say – I did not discuss it with the Doctor and for such and such a reason. He said that he cannot remember discussing it. It leaves a sense of depression.

The Judge has desisted. 'One more point: when you were talking about Mrs Morell's deterioration when you saw her in September, did you mean that you did *not expect* her to *get better*?'

One can almost hear the jury listen.

Dr Harris: 'Well, in cases like hers there are phases which could either be got over, or which might be the beginning of deterioration.'

('If Mrs Bardell were right, it was perfectly clear Mr Pickwick was wrong, and if they thought the evidence of Mr Clump worthy of credence they would believe it, and if they didn't why they wouldn't.')

And now for Dr Douthwaite. Dr Douthwaite must be six foot six. He is a most handsome man – profile, greying hair, handsome in the way of the good-looking soldier who has reached, perhaps, the rank of Lieutenant-General. Such an appearance is not unobtrusive, and the most striking thing about it is his height. Standing in the box, Dr Douthwaite stoops slightly and even so gives the impression that his head touches the canopy.

The Attorney-General [organ tone]: 'And you reside at number – Harley Street?'

'I do.'

'And you are a Senior Physician at Guy's Hospital?'

Dr Douthwaite: 'I am.'

They begin with the known causes of a stroke. Dr Douthwaite

explains that there are several – cerebral haemorrhage, a burst blood vessel; cerebral thrombosis, where there is a clot in an artery in the brain.

The Attorney-General: 'How long can life last after cerebral thrombosis?'

Dr Douthwaite [cheerful certainty]: 'For many years.'

'What was the cause of the stroke from which Mrs Morell suffered?'

[Trigger-quick] 'In all probability cerebral thrombosis.'

[Intoning] 'And what is the proper treatment for a patient who has suffered such a stroke?'

[Casually dogmatic] 'Within a few days, as soon as one is able to obtain cooperation of the patient, one should at once try to mobilize the patient and encourage movement of the body.' [Hearty] 'Massages, exercises, and so forth.'

The Attorney-General [continuing in monotone]: 'Is there in your opinion any justification for injecting morphia and heroin immediately after a stroke?'

[Coolly off-hand] 'No justification whatsoever.'

'Is it right or wrong to do so?'

'Wrong. In all circumstances wrong.'

Qualification, during the past days, had grown into a habit of thought; this has a ring of such absolute, such towering, such *natural* certainty that the court sits stunned.

The Attorney-General: 'What about morphia alone?'

'Morphia alone should not be given to someone who has had a stroke; unless there is an episode of acute mania, and then' [scornful toss] 'only a single injection.'

The Doctor is actually bouncing on his chair in anger, pinching his lips and shaking his head, an expression of obstinate mortification on his face, the look of a man who knows that he knows better.

[Blank drone] 'What would be the effect of morphia and heroin on an old lady who has had a stroke? Would it have an effect on her prospects of resuming normal life?'

[Cheerful ferocity] 'It would greatly interfere with her rehabilitation.'

(Back bench exchange of looks. The exasperated French shrug. '*Mais voyons, elle était au bout de sa vie, la pauvre dame. . . .*')

The Attorney-General: 'Is it necessary to use sedation immediately upon someone who has suffered a stroke?'

Dr Douthwaite [looking over his shoulder]: 'It is not necessary.'

'Is it desirable?'

'Not in general. I'm not referring to something given to ensure sleep.' [Still looking at some point in court] 'Sedation there is quite reasonable.'

The Attorney-General: 'When you talk of that, does it include morphia and heroin?'

'Completely *ex*clude.'

'With someone of this age who has suffered a stroke, is it necessary to keep the patient as quiet as possible in the day-time?'

Dr Douthwaite [running his hand down the side of his head, smoothing his hair]: 'No, not in day-time.'

'Is there a risk of another stroke if the patient is not kept as quiet as possible?'

[Blithe scorn] 'On the contrary. There is more risk of another stroke from thrombosis, for clotting is more likely to occur if the patient is kept very quiet.'

'Would you expect a patient suffering from stroke to exhibit signs of irritability?'

'I would expect a woman of her age to be suffering to some extent from arterio-sclerosis and this would lead to a degree of irritability.'

The Attorney-General [neutral tone]: 'And would that be a justification for administering morphia and heroin?'

'Oh no, completely contrary.' [Cold shrug] 'It would give rise to addiction; and certainly those drugs as such are not nearly as effective as much safer drugs for that purpose.'

'Were those drugs available in 1950?'

'Oh, yes.'

'Is morphia liable to produce addiction?'

'Very liable. The individual is likely to become addicted in a fortnight, certainly within three weeks.'

'What would be the addicted patient's attitude toward the doctor who is supplying the drug?'

[Hard clip] 'Dependence on the doctor.'

'For what legitimate purpose can morphia and heroin be daily administered over a prolonged period?'

[Promptly] 'Only for severe pain that cannot be quelled by any other means.'

'Can you tell us something about the normal dosage of morphia?'

'One-quarter of a grain. The British Pharmacopoeia gives the maximum dose as a third of a grain.'

Here the Judge proffers some lucid help. 'Mr Attorney – the normal dose, in *what* time?'

The Attorney-General: 'At what intervals is this maximum dose supposed to be given?'

Dr Douthwaite [nonchalant assurance]: 'To people in pain it could be given perhaps every four hours. If there were really agonizing pain, it might even be given every hour.'

The Attorney-General says that he now wishes to deal with heroin.

Dr Douthwaite makes a gesture indicating that he is all ears. 'Heroin is a stronger drug than morphia. It is more dangerous. Its action is similar to that of morphia but it differs in important respects. It powerfully depresses respiration.'

The Attorney-General: 'Can you give an idea how it compares with morphia in that respect?'

[Serenely] 'About three or four times as powerful.'

'What is the maximum dose?'

'According to the B.P. one-sixth grain. Heroin is seldom given more than once every six hours except in cases of terrible pain. It has very little sedative effect.'

The Attorney-General: 'What then is the effect of a routine dose of heroin?'

'The effect, very simply, is a craving for more. It supplies pleasurable excitement.'

'In your opinion, should heroin be given to old people?'

'No.'

'In any circumstances?'

Dr Douthwaite: 'It is axiomatic that people over seventy should not have heroin unless they are suffering from some incurable disease.'

Between his two warders, the Doctor sorrowfully wags his head.

'Can you tell us something about the process of drug addiction?'

After a period of administration, Dr Douthwaite says, people develop a tolerance. Once tolerance is acquired the drug has less and less effect and lasts a shorter time; larger doses have to be given to secure any effect at all. When the drugs are wearing off there is craving and excitability.

'What can one do about this acquired tolerance?'

'There are two courses.' [Resting his back against the box] 'You can stop the drug and the tolerance will disappear in a week or two; or you can increase the drug and immediately you will overcome the tolerance and satisfy the craving.'

The Attorney-General: 'What are the results of stopping the drug?'

Dr Douthwaite: 'The patient will be terribly ill and have acute pains in the limbs and collapse. This is the state of withdrawal.'

'We have heard from other witnesses about the twitchings suffered by Mrs Morell. Could they be produced by the administration of heroin?'

[Grim *allegro*] 'Oh, yes, they could!'

Then comes the short adjournment. Some of the special correspondents, unhardened yet to the see-saw of a case, are staggered and subdued; there is a sheepish feeling of having been caught footling.

'Dr Douthwaite, now I want to ask you about paraldehyde.'

'Its typical feature is its smell which is revolting.'

[Boom] 'Is it a sedative?'

'Yes.'

'Could it be used to endeavour to stop twitchings?' A deadly question delivered in the routine tone.

'Yes.'

'What would be the effect if it were superimposed on a heavy administration of morphia and heroin?'

[Hard] 'It would be likely to produce death.'

The Judge [clearing the air; matter of fact]: 'Is it by itself a dangerous drug?'

'No.'

'The immediate cause of Mrs Morell's death was certified by the Doctor as cerebral thrombosis. Are there any signs in the nursing reports that justify that conclusion?'

[Toss] 'None.'

'We know that another practitioner, Dr Fox, endorsed this. Can you tell whether a person died of cerebral thrombosis by external examination?'

Dr Douthwaite: 'You cannot.'

('*Quel acharnement quand même contre un confrère dans le malheur!*') Indeed, the expert's olympian implacability seems extraordinary.

The Attorney-General, fetching up the stock question, 'Is there any justification or legitimate ground in your view for administering heroin and morphia together?'

[Chin out] 'No.'

'What can be the medical object of giving a routine injection of morphia and heroin?'

'There isn't one!'

The Doctor, beet-red in the face, rocks to and fro.

The Attorney-General calls out for the nursing books and the pace slackens. [Quoting an entry for June 1950] 'How would you describe that dosage?' (1/3 grain heroin and 5/12 morphia.)

Dr Douthwaite: 'A very heavy dosage.'

[Referring to November 10th] ' "May have heroin one grain hourly if necessary."?'

Dr Douthwaite: 'A high dosage and an astonishing instruction!'

[November 12th (when 3 1/2 grains of heroin and 2 grains of morphia had been given in twenty-four hours)] 'Dr Douthwaite,

I want you to express your considered opinion as to the effect on the semi-paralysed lady of eighty-one of the dosage given in these last days, allowing for the tolerance acquired by the previous routine injections?'

'I believe it would have produced jerky convulsions, and ultimately death.'

The Attorney-General [dropping the prompter's manner. Very slowly and gravely]: 'What conclusion do you draw from the dosage administered in the last days, what conclusions do you draw as to the intentions with which that dosage must have been prescribed?'

Thick silence. Dr Douthwaite [in a quiet voice]: 'The only conclusion I can come to is that the intention on November 8th was to terminate her life.'

The Doctor alone is still swinging his head in mournful negation.

The prosecution does not leave it there.

'If it was true that she was given those two 5 c.c. injections on the night before she died, what would be the effect of this paraldehyde on top of the heroin?'

Dr Douthwaite [thin near-smile]: 'To make the heroin more lethal.'

DAY NINE

'*HOME?*'

'In the bag?'

'It's a walkover all right!'

'Do you think there is a doctor in England who will go into that box and stand up for heroin?'

'Dr Douthwaite was *very* sure.'

'Yes – I slept on it, too.'

'Can any man know that much?'

'Well, he is the great narcotics wallah.'

'Wait till Lawrence deals with him.'

'Yes; there's Mr Lawrence.'

'An international authority isn't a bunch of nurses who talked too much.'

Last night the defence had asked leave to postpone cross-examination till today; now, Mr Lawrence is on the brink of it.

The Judge is in his chair. Dr Douthwaite is in the box; Mr Lawrence has risen. Dr Douthwaite has the first word. He turns to the Attorney-General; he has been furnished, he says, with yesterday's transcript of his evidence and he has marked some errors. Mr Lawrence sits down again. The Attorney-General has marked some errors, too. Pages rustle. Together, they go over the typing mistakes. Ten minutes pass.

Mr Lawrence makes a movement. The prosecution has one or two more questions. At a quarter to eleven Mr Lawrence is able to go over the top.

'I want you to be quite clear' [unruffled *largo*] 'what your position to my Lord and the jury is in relation to the charge of murder. Have I understood it correctly in this way, that, as a doctor and a specialist yourself, you are saying the Doctor formed the intention to terminate life on November 8th and carried that intention into effect over the next five days?'

Dr Douthwaite [quietly]: 'Yes.'

'I think it follows from what you said yesterday that the murderous intent, in your view, was present in his mind from November 8th onwards to the end?'

'Yes.'

[*Adagio*] 'I hardly suppose you have often expressed a graver or more fateful opinion on a matter than that?'

'No.'

[*Vivace*] 'Before going into the witness-box and expressing that opinion, had you satisfied yourself that you had every piece of relevant evidence before you on which to judge?'

Assent.

Mr Lawrence: 'You gave evidence in this case before the magistrates?'

'I did.'

'When you gave evidence at that stage, you were entirely in ignorance of what her treatment by the Doctor had been before January 1950?'

'Yes.'

'And you gave your evidence partly on the hypothesis that for the last three or four days of her life this lady had been in a continuous coma?'

'Yes.'

[Quick thrust] 'This turned out on the facts to be quite wrong?'

'Yes, not a continuous coma.'

Mr Lawrence: 'Do you know where she had her stroke in July 1948?'

'In Cheshire, I understand, during a visit to her son.'

[Lively interest] 'Had you made any *inquiries* before giving evidence against the Doctor yesterday – had you made any inquiries yourself or asked anybody – about the symptoms of her stroke? the circumstances? the treatment she had in Cheshire?'

Dr Douthwaite: 'I have said in conferences it would be very interesting to know what treatment she had before she came under the care of the Doctor.'

Mr Lawrence [velvet claws]: 'Interesting in the sense that it would be *relevant* and *material* to the medical picture? And did you ask for this relevant and material information to be found, or attempts to be made to furnish you with it, before you reached your final conclusion?'

[Stiffly] 'I did not regard it as my duty to find out facts of that sort. The facts on which I am expressing an opinion are the facts that have been presented to this court.' [Pause] 'I was told that the information was not available.'

[Sharply] 'Who told you it was not available?'

'I'm not certain. It was at one of the conferences by a counsel for the Crown.'

[Pressing] 'It would be most *important* to know before condemning the Doctor's treatment from the start as you did yesterday what happened in Cheshire?'

[Coolly] 'It would be *interesting* to know what happened in Cheshire.'

Mr Lawrence [swinging to the Judge]: 'My Lord, I want the witness to look at a document – '

It *is* a copy of the nursing records of the Cheshire Hospital – Mr Lawrence has a second rabbit in his top hat. The next instant he is reading out aloud. ' "June 26th," that was her first day there, "luminal, two grains; slept very little." ' Glance at bench and jury. 'Mrs Morell was under the care of two doctors, a Dr Turner and a consultant, Dr Pemberton. "June 27th, poor night. Patient very distressed and complaining of severe pain." ' To Dr Douthwaite, 'The very phrase you were using rather freely yesterday. "Two veramon tablets given, but patient was unable to swallow them." ' [Reading straight on] ' "Morphia 1/4 grain given. Patient slept." '

The faintest pause, and he reads on briskly. Sure enough, during the whole of Mrs Morell's ten days at the Cheshire Hospital there is every night a record of a morphia injection.

[Sustained] 'Dr Douthwaite – from these records certain things at least are clear, are they not? First of all, she was a very ill woman? She complained of severe pain? After two nights of attempting to give her sleep by barbiturates, the doctors at the hospital resorted to morphia?'

'Yes.'

'And every night for the rest of her stay in that hospital and under those doctors she had morphia?'

'Yes.'

'And after these injections, there is some record of her having slept?'

'Yes.'

'What you were saying yesterday was this, no doctor should give morphia to a patient with a stroke, except in one instance only, that is, if the patient had acute mania, and then in one isolated injection.' [*Maestoso*] 'Does the field of condemnation that you are spreading from this witness-box include Dr Turner of Cheshire for having given the patient morphia after a stroke?'

Dr Douthwaite: 'If that was the treatment for the stroke, yes.'

'It does – ?' Mr Lawrence throws up his hands, 'Good gracious me!'

[Points of laughter.]

[Continuing detached] 'We are left with this: that three doctors – two of whom are not on a charge of murder at all – deliberately gave this particular patient injections of morphia, not single injections, but night after night. If I understand your position rightly, you are condemning as a matter of medical practice each of these doctors' use of morphia in this case?'

Dr Douthwaite: 'If it was used simply on account of the stroke.'

'The pain *was* a consequence of the stroke? You cannot have it both ways, can you?'

'We do not know where that pain was.'

'Do you think that is an answer to my question?' [Rationally] 'It does not matter in what part of the body the pain was, does it? the pain was a consequence of the stroke?'

Dr Douthwaite [leaning back in the box]: 'It is probable.'

[Controlled exasperation] 'Are you saying that this woman, who has what you admitted to be a pretty severe stroke, goes into a hospital and is then very distressed and complains of pain – are you really saying that the pain had nothing to do with the stroke?'

'It is possible, though not probable.'

Mr Lawrence [lively]: 'All these doctors, Dr Turner and Dr Pemberton, Dr Harris and the Doctor, every one of those saw the patient himself in the condition she was in at the time?'

'Yes.'

'So far as you know, *you* never saw Mrs Morell?'

'I agree.'

Mr Lawrence: 'As a general principle it is true, isn't it, only the man on the spot knows the full true picture? He has not got to be the perfect physician, the ideal that is stored up somewhere in heaven, or, indeed, in the mind of a Harley Street consultant?'

'.....'

Mr Lawrence [switching]: 'Could six to twelve months have been a reasonable prognosis in terms of expectation of life after her stroke?'

'Yes, I think it would.'

'Now the reasonable object of a general practitioner's treatment for what he could reasonably expect to be the remaining months of that woman's life would be to make her life as tolerable as it could be to her and as it could be to those who had to look after her?'

Dr Douthwaite [dryly]: 'The first object would be to restore her health.'

Mr Lawrence: 'That of course is the highest level. But no doctor in his senses would think that short of a miracle he could restore a woman of seventy-nine or eighty to her pre-stroke health?'

'Oh, no, I agree with that.'

[Cooperative tone] 'So what he's got to do is his reasonable best for what is left of her life?'

'Oh, yes.'

'And whatever you may say about the use of these drugs, the fact is – as recorded – that certainly until September this woman was being got up and about during the day-time?'

Dr Douthwaite: 'Certainly.' (And here is the reward of trotting out all those entries about surgical boots and wheel-chair drives.)

Mr Lawrence: 'The Doctor is a general medical practitioner, not a Harley Street specialist?'

'Yes.'

'Is it not necessary in relation to a murder charge to see the picture of the treatment as a whole?'

'Oh, quite.'

[*Andantino*] 'And by September 1950 she had already exceeded the reasonable prognosis for expectation of life by at least eighteen months or so?'

Something that could be taken for a faint superior smile crosses Dr Douthwaite's face.

Mr Lawrence: 'I do not see anything amusing in that, Dr Douthwaite. I hope you don't.'

'No, I quite agree. I was just thinking of your terms of prognosis.'

Mr Lawrence [deruffled; so many passages are like the uproarious and abortive onset of a dog-fight]: 'Now if you are dealing with a case where you are giving morphia either to deal with pain or some physically degenerated condition, the time will come when you won't be able to deal with what you are trying to deal with by means of a level dosage?'

'I agree.'

'And you are at the point where you find that you have to adopt one of two courses? One is to stop the drug, which in the case of an old woman verging on eighty might very well cause collapse with a risk of death?'

'Yes.'

'And the other course is to go on and give her more?'

'Yes – '

'That is exactly what Dr Harris did?'

'Yes.'

'With comparative success?'

'Yes – '

[Forging ahead] 'She was going downhill that September? She was reaching the terminal stage of her life?'

'Yes.'

'And as the irritation of this later stage was getting worse, her doctor would be faced with this dilemma of either having to stop the drugs and thus risk collapse, or giving increased doses of it? What to do in these circumstances is in fact one of the most difficult problems that face a doctor?'

Dr Douthwaite: 'Oh, yes.'

'Your objection to morphia and heroin is because of the liability of the patient to acquire addiction?'

[Some cheerful ferocity regained] 'That is *one* of my objections.'

'Is it fairly obvious that there is no perfect drug that has not got some disadvantage?'

'No, I agree.'

'If a general practitioner decides that he has to make use of some sort of drug he has got to balance up the advantages and disadvantages in his choice?'

'Certainly.'

Mr Lawrence: 'A short expectation of life very substantially minimizes or mitigates the dangers of addiction?'

'Yes.' [Warming] 'May I say this is a problem which often confronts us, and my practice in teaching has always been that if a patient is obviously dying it is ridiculous to worry about addiction. If the strong probability is that the patient will not live for more than a month or two, you cannot worry about addiction. If the prognosis is very doubtful about time, say, six months to five years, addiction should be carried in mind.'

Mr Lawrence [rounding it off]: 'So in the case of Mrs Morell one of the most prominent circumstances would be that the reasonable expectation of life at the time of her stroke was about six to twelve months?'

The Doctor, nursing books in front of him, has been listening with signs of satisfaction.

'A great deal more is known about drugs today than it was thirty years ago?'

'It is.'

'When the Doctor qualified in the early 1920s, morphia and heroin were commonly used as hypnotics?'

'Morphia was.'

'Not heroin?'

'Not commonly.'

Mr Lawrence: 'Can we put it this way – thirty or forty years ago both morphia and heroin, heroin perhaps to a lesser extent, were used as hypnotics and not exclusively in cases of severe pain?'

Dr Douthwaite: 'I accept that.'

'Would it surprise you if, in fact, at a high level in your profession both morphia and heroin are administered to people over seventy, and not only in cases of severe pain?'

'It would surprise me very much.'

Mr Lawrence: 'I put it to you that they are not dangerous if properly used?'

'I don't agree if you refer to heroin.'

[Earnestly] 'When we say loosely "these dangerous drugs", are we not expressing only one side of the picture? They are most beneficial drugs, are they not?'

'I agree.'

'Indeed, if properly used these opiates and opium derivatives have been regarded as one of the greatest blessings conferred on the medical profession?'

'Agreed.'

'You, in fact, led a deputation to the Home Office asking there should be no ban placed on the manufacture of heroin in this country?'

Dr Douthwaite: 'I was invited to join it and took a leading part.'

Counsel and witness appear to have entered a relaxed phase. Not that one can ever be sure.

'As we know, there are recorded instances of special injections given by the Doctor; have you tried to determine the character of these?'

Dr Douthwaite: 'I was not particularly interested in finding out about these. I was interested in the drugs that were prescribed as set out in the various summaries.'

Mr Lawrence: 'Can we disregard the special injections for all purposes in this case, in your view?'

'As far as I am concerned, yes.'

'Would you take it from me that the special injection in November is contemporaneous with a prescription at Browne's for a caffeine capsule specially made up?'

'I will certainly take it from you if you say so.'

Mr Lawrence: 'Caffeine is a stimulant and an antidote to morphia?'

'A feeble antidote.'

[Gathering momentum] 'Would it not have been odd for a doctor with murderous intent to have given an antidote – however feeble – at the same time as a morphia injection?'

[Lightly] 'Agreed.'

Mr Lawrence [cocking his head]: 'You are not suggesting – are you? – there was any murderous intent in the Cheshire hospital when she was started on morphia?'

[Veneer of patience] 'No.'

The morning wears on; and the afternoon. As the hours pass, Dr Douthwaite seems to be growing taller in the box. He is not spared a single point. Mrs Morell *was* alert and talkative after those special injections? Apparently . . . Drugs *are* less dangerous if there is some tolerance already present? Less dangerous, yes. ... *This* patient *had* acquired increased tolerance? She had. ... Hence *need* to increase the dosage? Dr Douthwaite stoops and sways and stretches in his cage. ... And nurses – experienced nurses, not young probationers – thought her symptoms those of senile deterioration? Well, says Dr Douthwaite, by and large they were. ... Discretion was given to those nurses over and over again to use those injections? Yes. ... The Doctor even stopped morphia at one time and gave only heroin, trying *variation* instead of increase – didn't it look as if that was what he was doing there?

'I don't know what was in the Doctor's mind.'

[All hands out] 'Did you not before? When you saw murderous intent?'

Dr Douthwaite is silent.

Will he look at the result of this variation? She is not sleeping badly, eating better. ... Not such a bad result is it? On November 3rd they have the son's visit. Mrs Morell is lachrymose and sullen; the nurse telephoned the Doctor and he prescribed a quarter grain of heroin. That *was* the right thing to do?

'Yes.'

Then the restlessness increased, there were more frequent doses of heroin; the Doctor had to go back to morphia again. Not unusual to continue with a drug the patient is used to?

Dr Douthwaite: 'Not at all.' Then, on his own, 'Curious, she was asleep a quarter of an hour after an injection of hyperduric morphia, very curious. ... '

They have reached the last days. Mr Lawrence [reading]: ' "Restless all the time in a quieter way. Not sleeping." And then we see the signal, "Getting restless and aggressive", and then the nurse gives another injection?'

'Yes, I see.'

'And that was the situation which confronted the general practitioner on the morning of November 8th?'

Assent.

Mr Lawrence: 'He visited her at half past eleven, and if you are right, formed the intention to murder her?'

Dr Douthwaite [shrugging]: 'Yes.'

'November 9th. Let us see. This is the second day of the murderous period. See what this murderous doctor did. It is clear from this record – I don't think I have missed anything – that the only sleep she had during the whole of that day and the following day was fifteen minutes at eight o'clock in the morning and twenty minutes after lunch?'

'Very well.'

Mr Lawrence: 'If this sleeplessness would have been allowed to go on, she would have collapsed eventually?'

'Yes.' Then, for no apparent reason, in sudden weariness perhaps with consistency, Dr Douthwaite says as if for himself, 'Heroin *is* useful – I remember a woman of seventy-three who had it prescribed.'

Mr Lawrence [quickly]: 'So it is sometimes prescribed – ?'

Dr Douthwaite, chafing against the box, says nothing.

[Driving on] 'In view of what had gone on – over years – the Doctor couldn't cut her off from what she'd been having, could he? He *had* to go with it and increase it? He *could not* cut her off because that would have meant death?'

'Yes, at this stage.'

Mr Lawrence: 'Now look at the next report. The patient was confused and talkative, the Doctor saw her at 10 p.m., he gave her an injection of hyperduric morphia and she slept for six hours. Do you notice the selection of that type of morphia?'

'I do.'

'It is a slow-acting type, is it not?'

'It is.'

'On the eve of murder – a slow-acting drug? A strange choice for a murderer?'

Dr Douthwaite shrugs.

'And on this same day we see that he also gave her some atropine. Now let me read you this.' [From a marked place in a bulky tome] ' "Atropine is classed as an antidote to morphia, and it is sometimes given in conjunction with morphia and to offset some of the effects of morphia like vomiting and constipation." ' Looking up, 'So on the second day on which you are saying the Doctor carried out his murderous intention, she was given on his instructions an injection which contained an ingredient which is an antidote to morphia?'

[Negligently] 'Oh, yes.'

'Had you realized that fact?'

[Frosty] 'Yes. The purpose for which atropine is usually given with morphia is to reduce dryness in the throat. It was a very weak solution.'

Mr Lawrence: 'Here is the man who was murdering her, giving, however weak it might be, an antidote?'

Dr Douthwaite [like a tip in the smallest permissible coin]: 'Yes.'

'It was the Doctor's duty to produce sleep. But sleep was no longer produced, those drugs were no longer working, in other words their hypnotic value had gone?'

'Yes, completely.'

'And then he tried one more variation.' [Lightly] 'On the last night he tried paraldehyde. Which clearly was one of the safest remedies for insomnia, one of the safest there is?'

Dr Douthwaite: 'Agreed.'

'And 5 c.c. is quite a common dose? Even another 5 c.c. would still be within permissible limits?'

'Quite.'

'Could anything else have been given in this last stage?'

'He might have given hyoscine.'

'Anything else?'

Dr Douthwaite: 'There are several others that could have been given with safety.'

Mr Lawrence [silky]: 'Including paraldehyde?'

'Including paraldehyde,' says Dr Douthwaite.

The court rises. As the Doctor vanishes down his manhole, one has a glimpse of his face wreathed in an open smile.

DAY TEN

'I AM not inviting a Harley Street opinion about the skill of a G.P. I know what your view has been over these last days.' Mr Lawrence is winding up yesterday's work. [*Rallentando*] 'But at least it is a possible alternative that this G.P. was following a consistent course with these drugs to produce the result which it was his duty to produce?' [Stops out] 'Dr Douthwaite, there is no *necessity* to postulate a murderous intent?'

[Firmly] 'In the first place, with great respect, where I live has nothing to do with my knowledge or opinions.' [Low voice] 'I *have* given evidence of intent to terminate life.'

Mr Lawrence: 'What I put to you is this – that on the factual history, there is *no need* to postulate an intent to murder?'

Dr Douthwaite [quietly]: 'I am forced to postulate that on the drugs given in the last days in November.'

[Rationally, forcefully] 'If you will not come the whole way with me, at any rate you will come some of the way in agreeing to a *possible* alternative view? You would conceive it is quite possible, would you not, that another doctor might not find himself forced to the same conclusion?'

'*Yes* – we all have different opinions.'

Again it is in the smallest acceptable coin, and one cannot very well see how Dr Douthwaite could have got out of giving it; nevertheless, it leaves a door open, and Mr Lawrence keeps it at that.

The atmosphere has changed since Wednesday afternoon when Dr Douthwaite made his first appearance. Dogmatic gloom, to some extent, has lifted; instead, there is now a sense of doubt and muddle. It is Dr Douthwaite's attitude that seems as perplexing at the moment as the whole question of the Doctor's innocence or guilt.

The Attorney-General rises; the court is ready for the next attempt to push the pendulum.

First point. When the Doctor took over after Cheshire, he increased the morphia she had been given there and also added heroin. [Turning to Dr Douthwaite] 'Can this be properly described as merely following the Cheshire medication?'

'Of course not.'

'My learned friend has asked you a great number of questions about the necessity of securing sleep at all costs. Was there, in fact, any shortage of sleep?' [Reading selected extracts from the nursing books] ' "Five hours – five and a half – Six hours – Seven – " ' [Arched eyebrows] 'Any shortage of sleep so far – ? For an old lady, bed-ridden, she had plenty of sleep?'

Dr Douthwaite: 'Oh, yes.'

'What about this so-called doctor's dilemma?'

Dr Douthwaite: 'There *are* drugs which can be used to get a patient gradually off heroin and morphia.'

The Attorney-General: 'Would there have been a risk?'

'No risk, if it had been attempted early enough.'

Mrs Morell's longevity.

The Attorney-General: 'When her first expectation of life had been fulfilled to the maximum, and even exceeded, was there not now a new lease, a high expectation of life to be prognosticated?'

'Oh yes.'

Medical sense? Mathematical sense? Common sense?

'How would you qualify the dosages prescribed?'

Dr Douthwaite [hurling it through the court]: 'Colossal.'

The Attorney-General [deep boom]: 'Has anything said in this court affected your opinion as to the death of Mrs Morell?'

[Melancholy tinge] 'No.'

[Weighted] 'To what do you attribute her death?'

[Quick big drum] 'Drugs, probably assisted by paraldehyde. In the absence of paraldehyde, in my opinion, the morphia and heroin administered on the last few days would have killed her.'

The Judge [modestly]: 'I would like to ask the witness some questions.'

Dr Douthwaite turns to the bench.

'Before the jury can convict they must be satisfied that there is an act of murder. In the circumstances of this case it means that the Doctor either administered the drugs himself with intent to kill or gave directions to the nurses that he hoped and intended would, if carried out, kill the patient. Now I think I am right in saying that the Doctor paid seventeen visits to Mrs Morell in the period between November the 8th and 12th, and on all or most of these occasions he either administered drugs himself or left directions for the nurses as to what they were to do. If the case of the Crown is right, then one or more of these acts was attempted murder, and I should like to be able to assist the jury by pointing out to them precisely what in relation to each act it is that forces you to postulate murder was being committed or attempted.'

Dr Douthwaite: 'I may have to postulate it in relation to the doses that had gone before, or, more exactly, in relation to the doses that were *not* given.' [Settling down to explain] 'She was given no morphia from the 1st of November to the 5th, the days when only heroin was given. By withdrawing morphia from her for five days, he would certainly reduce the acquired tolerance to it. I wondered what was the possible reason, and that is why I did not make up my mind on the probable desire to terminate life until I saw that the return to morphia on November 6th was followed by a rapid increase together with large doses of heroin. Clearly this was not an attempt to wean her from addiction, a late realization of what was happening. If it had been so, why should not the heroin be reduced first rather than the morphia? My conclusions after that were based on the rapidly mounting doses and very large doses of the last five days.'

The Judge: 'Are you saying the morphia was deliberately withheld in order that it might be reintroduced fatally?'

Dr Douthwaite: 'That is what it appears to me, because I can see no other reason for it. There was no attempt at any substitution.'

There has been no hint of any of this before. The court can but sit, wait, listen, and try to trust their ears.

The Judge [calmly; with the evident intention to sort this out]: 'When you consider a doctor's method or treatment, would the very last thing you would think of be murder?'

[Blankly] 'Quite true, my Lord.'

(Back bench: 'First thing he was asked to look for. That's why they hired him, didn't they?')

The Judge: 'You would explore every other hypothesis before?'

'Yes.'

[Settling down] 'Let me invite you to consider this. You criticize the Doctor's treatment? He embarked upon the wrong line from the beginning?'

'In my opinion, he had.'

'But murder is not suggested as an explanation of that?'

Dr Douthwaite: 'No.'

'The alternative explanation would seem to be that he did not understand the right use of dangerous drugs?'

'That *could* be concluded. *I* cannot believe that a medical man of his experience and qualifications is not aware of the action of those two drugs.'

The Judge: 'He may have the wrong ideas. . . . He may have old-fashioned ideas. . . . Is this a possibility?'

'Yes, it is *possible*. I do not think he would not know the dangers of morphia and heroin.'

'Is it possible that he might have thought – however wrongly in your view, and in spite of the dangers – that it *was* the right treatment to give?'

Dr Douthwaite: 'He might have thought so, I suppose, in the early stages.'

'Therefore you start with a man who is taking a wrong line of treatment not for sinister reasons, but because he is not taking the right line?'

'Yes.'

'Are you prepared to postulate that when he reintroduced the morphia on November 6th he must have intended to kill?'

'I am.'

The Judge: 'He did *not* kill as a result of that, so the next day the injection is increased to half a grain?'

'Yes.'

'And he also left instructions that the same doses might be repeated during the night?' [No expression] 'Can I take it that in giving those instructions he was making sure, as it were, that if the first doses did not work, doses would be given during the night until it did work?'

Dr Douthwaite: 'Yes.'

The Judge: 'And the next morning he finds the patient is not dead, so he gives a special injection? But I think you said you disregarded the special injections?'

'I had to. I do not know what they were.'

'Well – he finds that she is not dead and he leaves instructions that she might have half a grain of morphia and half a grain of heroin if necessary. He is carrying on with what you say can only be a lethal dose?'

'Yes.'

The Judge: 'Then he makes his third visit in the evening. He finds she has not had any dose during the day, it had not turned out to be necessary. So he gives an injection of heroin and hyperduric morphia, and directs that it should be repeated if necessary. Do you attach any appreciable importance to the change to hyperduric morphia?'

'No appreciable importance.'

'So he is trying again a lethal dose, in your view, and leaving instruction for the lethal dose to be repeated?'

Dr Douthwaite says, yes.

Coolly, the Judge continues piling it on. 'Then he visits her again on the next day, November 9th – She is still alive – He gives her one grain of morphia – Would *that* be a dose intended to kill?'

In the circumstances, yes. The Doctor is carrying on knowing that there must be a steady accumulation of drugs.

'And he leaves behind him instructions to give a grain of heroin s.o.s. And you would say that this grain of heroin might well have been fatal – ?'

Dr Douthwaite says, yes.

'Then he visits her again the next morning – this is the eighth visit – he gives her half a grain of morphia and she falls asleep. That half-grain – the only conclusion you can draw with regard to that is that he intended to kill?'

'That is my view.'

There seems nothing for it but to go on. Next morning, another visit, another injection, directions left to change the dose to half a grain of morphia and heroin each. 'Doctor, do you regard this combination as any more or less lethal?'

Dr Douthwaite: 'Oh, yes, indeed, the combination is more lethal.'

'Then the Doctor comes again in the evening and finds that the lethal dose has not worked, so he doubles it to one whole grain each of morphia and heroin, which' [looking at Dr Douthwaite] 'is the largest injection so far?'

'Yes, my Lord.'

[Dispassionately] 'How soon might he have expected that dose to work and bring about death?'

'It would add to the accumulation, so one would expect death within two or three days. . . . '

The Judge [mildly]: 'The medical picture appears to show that he was giving rather more doses than were really necessary?'

'Yes, my Lord.'

'Might he not reasonably have waited a few days to see the result without giving more?'

'He might well have.'

The Doctor's presence tends to get forgotten for hours on end, yet here he is, mute and round, on his chair in the middle of everything. How refreshing it would be if he were to lift his voice then and there, how convenient, how simple, how fitting; but in practice how double-edged and chaotic.

The Judge: 'Now we come to the last day and the fourteenth visit, when she had an injection of paraldehyde. You said at one time that it made death certain, if death were not certain already? In your view, it *was* certain?'

'Yes.'

'In a matter of days?'

'Yes.'

'The Doctor gave the paraldehyde because he was tired of waiting for the other drugs to act?'

Dr Douthwaite: 'Yes. A small injection of paraldehyde could have been given for an innocent purpose, but the 5 c.c. was meant to kill.'

The Judge: 'Does it really matter then whether the second injection of paraldehyde about which there has been a great deal of dispute was given or not?'

'No.'

The Judge: 'I think I have the picture quite clear now in my mind. Your view, if I may summarize it for the jury, is really this – that the first time the design for murder emerges from the medical pattern is when the Doctor drops the morphia and concentrates on the heroin? The only medical explanation for that being that he intends to reintroduce morphia with lethal effects? And then and thereafter all the subsequent injections, any one of them, could have been lethal and can only be explained on the basis that they were intended to be so? And that goes on until he takes to paraldehyde to bring about her death more quickly?' The Judge looks at Dr Douthwaite as if for final confirmation.

Dr Douthwaite says blankly, 'Yes, my Lord.'

After Dr Douthwaite has stepped down there is a baffled moment, a-bristle with postponed questions, while the case moves on. (The courts, so ungrudging of their time in many respects, are unwilling to waste half minutes of it sitting back.) The Crown call their other medical expert, the last hour of the Procrustean day is filled; but attention lags behind. The Judge, always alert to the unresolved, speaks to Mr Lawrence: 'You have heard me this afternoon ask a number of questions and get certain answers. . . . I do not regard it as part of my duty to cross-examine any witness. . . . I was struck by certain divergences between some of the answers given to me and answers given previously to you. If in these circumstances you were to make an application to cross-examine further, I would be inclined to grant it.'

Mr Lawrence asks whether he might consider the position over the week-end adjournment; he assumes that Dr Douthwaite will be here on Monday? And this prospect of beginning once more in the middle ends the second week of the trial.

THE THIRD WEEK

THE DEFENCE

DAY ELEVEN

THE defence have decided to take another chance. Dr Douthwaite is once more confronting Mr Lawrence.

'I want first of all to understand the theory of murder which you were explaining to my Lord on Friday.' His tone is completely hard. 'Am I right in thinking that it is really made up of two limbs? The first limb being that the Doctor withdrew morphia for some days in order to reduce the tolerance? and the second that he reintroduced morphia and thereafter gave increasing doses in conjunction with heroin to bring about a fatal result?'

Dr Douthwaite [equally cool]: 'Yes.'

'You know quite well, don't you, that the dosage during the last five days was well within the experience of general practitioners in terminal stages of illness without producing fatality?'

Dr Douthwaite says he would like to have a look at the summary before answering the question. Then, with a very slight, thin-lipped smile, 'There were five grains of heroin on November 11th, and that is thirty-five times the normal maximum dose.'

Mr Lawrence: 'It is no use taking one day in isolation without looking to what has gone before to see what the tolerance might be?' (Actually, the figure itself must be vastly misleading. The normal maximum dose, as stated, being 1/6 grain every 6 hours, 5 grains in 24 hours is not 35 times that dose, but 7½ times.) 'What I am putting to you is this – if this had been a case of a patient suffering from a spinal carcinoma, for example, the picture of that dosage complete over those days would have been one well within the experience of the profession?'

Dr Douthwaite still surprises by saying, 'It would have been a dosage suggesting a desire to terminate life.'

Mr Lawrence [blinking]: 'You would be driven into the witness-box to say that the G.P. who followed that course was a murderer, would you?'

'I would say he was giving large doses of drugs and those drugs would have caused death.'

Mr Lawrence: 'Would you mind facing the question and giving me an answer? You would not say in those circumstances that the general practitioner was a murderer?'

'No.'

The Judge leans forward: 'Do you say you would be forced to the conclusion that he intended to kill?'

Dr Douthwaite: 'Yes, my Lord. When I was asked earlier, I deliberately said that the drugs were given to terminate life. I do not know whether that is synonymous with murder. I did not introduce the word myself.'

Bench and counsel look at each other. 'It may be there is a question of law tied up with your question, Mr Lawrence?'

Mr Lawrence: 'Murder, Dr Douthwaite, is killing with intention of killing or terminating life.'

Evidently this is not as simple as it sounds. The Judge takes over for a minute and skirts, very lightly, one of the undercurrents of the case. 'I am anxious there should not be introduced into this now questions that may be partly questions of law. It may be a matter of law, I don't know, and it may be a matter of medical practice, that if a doctor gives drugs knowing that they will shorten life, but gives them because they were necessary to relieve severe pain, he is not committing murder.'

Mr Lawrence: 'Let me follow, if I may say so with respect, that very helpful comment from my Lord. This was a case of senile deterioration and in the last days the patient was suffering acute distress and lack of sleep. Would a doctor dealing with this case not be in the same position as the doctor who was dealing with acute pain in the final stages of an inoperable disease?'

Dr Douthwaite: 'I disagree. I think I have made it clear that this distress, especially these terrible twitchings the nurse told us about, were largely the result of drugs.' [Pause] 'Your example of someone in terrible pain is quite another matter. There is a profound difference between the acute pain in the terminal stages of an inoperable disease and the terminal stages of arterio-sclerosis.'

Mr Lawrence: 'Is the sole difference between the two cases this, in your opinion, that in the inoperable case the use of drugs would be justified because of the presence of pain, and in the other case not justified because there was only distress which falls short of severe pain?'

[Clear tone] 'Yes.'

Mr Lawrence: 'You are entitled to your opinion, but it is the doctor on the spot who has to judge in relation to his patient?'

[Amiably off-hand] 'I quite agree.'

[Bringing out the transcript of Day Ten] 'Would it be a fair summary of your view that *every* dose, of *whatever* size or kind, had been an attempt to terminate life?'

Dr Douthwaite: 'I think that is putting it a little bit inaccurately. I agree that every dose was given with a definite intent, but I don't want to give the impression that I thought each dose was expected in itself to kill.'

The Judge: 'What you were inferring was that the Doctor refrained from giving a dose of itself lethal because he thought it was too difficult and might arouse suspicion, and so he had to give a series of doses over a period, the combined effect of which he knew would kill?'

The Doctor shakes his head.

Dr Douthwaite: 'That is exactly what I mean! The drugs were given to an individual who was saturated with them. These drugs would accumulate in the body.'

Mr Lawrence: 'Dr Douthwaite, is this based on what is called the theory of accumulation?'

'It is.'

'Is it not a well-known fact that both morphia and heroin are notable for being non-accumulative drugs?'

'In the normal person, yes.'

'They are drugs which are eliminated relatively quickly, are they not?'

'Yes. We believe they are destroyed in the liver.'

'Dr Douthwaite, there is no reason at all then to postulate there was any accumulation in the body of this person?'

[Negligently, contemptuously] 'Yes, there is every reason.'

'Can you ever say precisely what accumulation of morphia there may be in a body?'

'No.'

'It is all speculation?'

'The nearer a patient is to death, the more accumulation will occur. . . . I cannot say more.'

Mr Lawrence: 'This woman *was* in the terminal stages of life in this last fortnight?'

'Yes.'

'Dying anyhow?'

'Well – she was dying.'

The Judge: 'Do you mean she was dying before November 1st?'

Dr Douthwaite: 'Yes, my Lord.'

Mr Lawrence stiffens. 'Let us come to the first limb of the theory you put forward to my Lord on Friday.' His tone is freezing and at the same time grave, and he really is most formidable, more so even than when he was bearing down on the nurses or sparring with the superintendent. 'The Doctor deliberately withdrew morphia on October 31st so that the patient should be rendered more vulnerable?'

'Yes.'

'Do you still adhere to that?'

[Meaning it] 'Yes.'

'By stopping this morphia over those five days he was, so to speak, removing the shield of protection from the larger doses which she had acquired?'

'Yes, he was removing that shield.'

[Great weight] 'And that was done deliberately?'

Dr Douthwaite: 'It was done deliberately.'

'With the conscious intention of reintroducing morphia with lethal effect?'

'So it appears.'

Mr Lawrence [very slowly, suavely, cuttingly]: 'When did you first think of this theory, Dr Douthwaite?'

[Not giving] 'Well, I presume it was when I studied the summary and the medical reports of the case.'

[Stress on every word] 'Before or after you first got into the witness-box to give evidence to the jury?'

'I think afterwards.'

[Whip-quick] 'When?'

'I cannot remember.'

[Sustained] 'Up to that point on Day Ten when my Lord started asking you questions, not a single hint of that theory had emerged from your lips?'

'I accept that.'

[Lashing out] 'The truth is that all this business is an afterthought on your part?'

'No, that is not true. As I said to my Lord I have been puzzled by the withdrawal.'

'That, Dr Douthwaite, is a part of your evidence which never emerged until my Lord himself asked you questions at the end of hours and hours of examination-in-chief, of cross-examination, and re-examination?'

'True.'

'In any case the medical theory upon which it is based is absolute rubbish, isn't it?'

[Sensation]

Dr Douthwaite does not answer.

Mr Lawrence [making good]:' You know quite well that morphia and heroin are drugs which are both of the same chemical and physiological kind?'

'Very similar.'

And Mr Lawrence brings out what has been on one's mind, that both are derivatives of opium and that there is in fact a cross-tolerance between them. 'And of all the degrees of cross-tolerance, the one between morphia and heroin is the highest?' Again Mr Lawrence has not spent an idle Saturday to Monday. 'And cross-tolerance means this – if you take morphia and acquire a tolerance to it, you are acquiring also a tolerance to its chemical ally, heroin?'

'To some degree, yes.'

'To some *considerable* degree?'

'Yes.'

'And vice-versa?'

'And vice-versa, yes.'

Mr Lawrence [growing in his shoes]: 'So this was *not* the case of a man withdrawing a drug to reduce tolerance and the patient not getting a chemically similar drug?'

Dr Douthwaite [no expression]: 'No.'

[Pressing on] 'The whole of this theory of yours is based on the supposition that this withdrawal of morphia would so greatly reduce her tolerance as to render the later doses lethal?'

'The reduction would make the morphia reintroduced more likely to be lethal.'

It no longer holds water, and the spectacle of the witness clinging to it is disconcerting.

Mr Lawrence [not letting up]: 'We can see from the nursing reports, can we not, that over the first three or four days of no morphia there are no withdrawal symptoms? Bearing in mind that you would naturally search for some innocent explanation before you went to the other, you cannot say that you were forced inescapably to place a sinister interpretation on this alteration in the drugging, can you?'

'Well, I can only say I see no explanation for it.'

Mr Lawrence [implacably]: 'The truth of this matter, Dr Douthwaite, is that you first of all gave evidence of one possibility to support the charge of murder, and then thought of something else after you had started?'

'I was turning it over in my mind and then it crystallized.'

[Cruising] 'But that is your personal view. You can conceive it quite possible that a reasonably minded physician of equal eminence might by no means find it necessary to postulate an intention to terminate life on the same evidence?'

'I have always agreed that there might be contrary medical opinion.' [Grim smile] 'I am expecting it.'

'And that would be medical opinion entitled to as much weight as yours?'

'I do not question that.'

Mr Lawrence [setting the seal on it]: 'You therefore admit the possibility of a skilled genuine view to the contrary of your position?'

This is no idle dotting of i's; for where there can be a valid contrary view, there is reasonable doubt and therefore, potentially, acquittal.

Dr Douthwaite [deadpan]: 'Yes.'

Mr Lawrence sits down. It is over.

The Attorney-General: 'Have you changed your opinion about the intent of which you have spoken?'

'No.'

'Has it altered at all as to the causes of death?'

'No.'

'Are the variations of doses in the last days consistent with an innocent intent?'

'No.'

'I am not quite sure I have understood your last answer to Mr Lawrence, which was that you accepted the possibility of a skilled genuine view contrary to yours?'

It is Dr Douthwaite's twelfth hour in the box.

'I meant by that, my Lord, that doctors frequently disagree. I *would* in fact be surprised if an eminent doctor disagreed with me on certain points.'

The Judge: 'If another doctor were to say he disagreed entirely with your views on accumulation, would that be a skilled genuine view to the contrary?'

Dr Douthwaite [with a touch of his cheerful certainty]: 'I can only say I really would be astonished if he did.'

'Your inference that there was an intent to kill on the Doctor's part depends upon your attribution to him of the knowledge that a single dose, not dangerous in itself, would be lethal because of the accumulation of drugs in the body?'

'Yes.'

The Judge: 'Before you were driven to that conclusion, you had reviewed and excluded error, ignorance, and incompetence?'

[Convinced] 'Yes.'

'Could a view contrary to yours on the subject be due to error, ignorance, or incompetence, but be *honestly* held?'

Dr Douthwaite: 'Yes.'

'Then why do you postulate an intent to kill?'

'I cannot conceive a man with the Doctor's special qualifications having ignorance of this sort.'

The Judge: 'You mean that in the case of a G.P. it might be due to error, ignorance, or incompetence, but in the case of a G.P. *with* an anaesthetist's qualifications it could not be due to these?'

'That is my view.'

'It must follow then that if the Doctor were to go into the witness-box and say, "I disagree entirely with this view", he would be guilty of perjury – he would be saying he held a view which he cannot honestly hold?'

Dr Douthwaite: 'You have put me a very difficult point, my Lord. *No* – the Doctor could not honestly say so.'

'If any other doctor who is qualified goes into the witness-box and says that, your answer would be the same? that he honestly cannot say that?'

[Firmly] 'That would be my answer.'

The Judge: 'You say the treatment *could not* have been due to error, ignorance, or incompetence and *must* have been due to an intent to kill?'

[Stolidly] 'That is my view.'

The Judge: 'It must follow that anybody who expresses a view contrary to yours is expressing a view he cannot honestly hold?'

Dr Douthwaite: 'Yes.'

[Showing no expression] 'It is very important to see how far you go. . . . It would be quite easy for a medical man in your position to say, "I am saying no more about this treatment by the Doctor than that I think it was wrong and dangerous, and I think it caused death; but whether it was administered through error, ignorance, or incompetence or intent to kill is not for me to say and I am not going to say it." That is evidence you could have given, but you are going further and saying it *could* not have been due to error, ignorance, or incompetence but it *must* have been due to an attempt to kill.'

Dr Douthwaite [steadily]: 'That is so.'

The Judge: 'One more point. You said that it was clear to the Doctor that she was a dying woman on November 1st. Now this is quite outside your province, but I am telling you so that you follow what is in my mind: the jury may have to consider what motive the Doctor had. One motive that has been suggested is that if she had lived long enough she might have altered her will and deprived him of the benefits he had, or thought he had, under the will. So would you review the position at the end of October, if you can, to help the jury? If a man had that sort of motive would he have said, "Well, she has only a month to live anyway, or two months or three months"? How far would a doctor, seeing the medical picture as you see it, have felt it worthwhile to shorten her life for a purpose of that sort?'

'From the medical picture I would have expected her to have lived only for a matter of a few weeks, and probably no more than two months.'

'Is the Doctor saying to himself, "She can only live for three weeks anyway"? And would he be embarking then on a course that in fact took thirteen days to bring about her death?'

'He might well have.' And these are Dr Douthwaite's last words in the case.

After the short adjournment, the Crown call the last prosecution witness, their second medical expert, Dr Michael George Corbett Ashby, also of Harley Street, consultant neurologist to six London hospitals. He had already made a brief appearance on Friday afternoon at the fag end of Day Ten. He seems, at first glance, a professional man of young middle-age, cautious, serious, colourless, possibly both highly-strung and controlled. If one had to guess Dr Ashby's profession one might plump for research – medicine or science – without giving first choice to either.

The Attorney-General has disposed of the stock points: Dr Ashby has never found morphia and heroin prescribed together where there is no severe pain; he thinks that every G.P. must be well aware of the facts of morphia as it is a drug in almost universal use, but this need not necessarily be the case with heroin. Dr Ashby does not skimp his answers and there is a sense of thought behind them. One very much wonders how his evidence will square with Dr Douthwaite's.

The Attorney-General: 'Dr Ashby, I want you to look at the clinical picture of the beginning after Cheshire. Could the quarter grain of morphia she was given there every night have produced addiction?'

Dr Ashby: 'I don't think it is possible to answer that with a straight yes or no.' [With a tentativeness that denotes its own kind of assurance] 'I believe it wouldn't be right to say that there wasn't the beginning of addiction in a very mild way.' At the end of a fourteen-day period it would be universal practice for doctors to review administration of morphia; just at the time he would have thought morphia would have been stopped or tailed off, it was doubled.

The Attorney-General [slow bowling]: 'Do you conceive any condition which would have necessitated this?'

'No. ... Especially not the addition of heroin as there was already danger of addiction and heroin is the most dangerous drug for that. ... I have studied the nurses' reports; in my opinion the patient was clearly well enough to be given some of the short-acting barbiturates to secure sleep and at the same time wean her, and yet I saw no sign of any such attempt.' [Pause] 'I listened with great attention to the problem as to what was the latest time at which what has been called the doctor's dilemma could have been resolved. My own conclusions are not in agreement with Dr Douthwaite that all was lost by November 1st. I was a bit surprised.'

(The French, who have been sent across the Channel by their editors in expectation of better things, are getting refractory.

'*Si au moins ils gueulaient* ...'

'*C'est d'un* calme ...'

'*D'un* poli ...'

'*C'est mortel.*'

'*Pourquoi ils ne se mettent pas à secouer un peu l'accusé?*'

'*Ils sont mous.*'

'*Eh bien non, c'est plutôt le genre de la maison.*')

Dr Ashby: 'I think there was just a faint chance of weaning her during the first week of November – it was a matter of either inevitable death or a faint chance. Speaking personally, it was a chance which ought properly to have been taken.'

'And when that last chance had gone, were the drugs administered after that in any degree a cause of her death or not?'

Dr Ashby: 'Oh, very largely.'

The Attorney-General: 'Were they, in your opinion, given for any purpose of improving the health of the patient?'

[Slowly] 'I think that once it has been established that a patient is dying, considerations of improving his health scarcely apply and a doctor must give his first thought to a patient's comfort and well-being. But, assuming there was no pain suffered at that time, I can see no justification for the doses given after November 8th. Perhaps "no justification" is too strong. The right course would have been to carry on with what may have been the necessary doses of the previous week to keep the patient in a hypnotic state.'

The Attorney-General [straight mono-drone]: 'Do you have anything to say about the withdrawal of morphia on October 31st?'

[Strained attention.]

Dr Ashby: 'I must say first of all that it did not cross my mind that this was anything sinister. I had noticed the morphia stopping. But it had not struck me that it might be an act calculated to produce the patient's death. The only effect I expected – in so far as morphia is a better sedative than heroin – was that of making the patient more irritable.'

The Attorney-General: 'On what do you base your view that after November 8th she was a dying woman?'

Dr Ashby [cautious, weary, grey]: 'Well, even that may be wrong. There may have been a faint chance even beyond that. I think we shall have to examine the books for these last five days.'

DAY TWELVE

ANOTHER field day for the tortoise. At the end of it there is one moment when it looks as if Mr Lawrence had put the prosecution case into a sieve. We start off with a sense of staleness: it's been going on too long; there are no hard facts; the old points have been churned into impenetrable mud. . . . Then Dr Ashby turns out to be a giving witness. One did not have the chance before to take his measure – interested, good-tempered, painstaking, willing to think and not afraid to hesitate, more anxious always to dissect a view than to present it. After some little time in the box he puts his hands in his pockets and keeps them there.

Dr Ashby holds the stand all day. The Attorney-General takes the best part of the morning; the cross-examination lasts till nearly tea-time; there are another ten minutes with the Judge, and that brings us in substance to the end of the case for the prosecution.

Weary rustle – the Attorney-General has invited court and witness to follow him through the nursing reports. Questions trudge from point to well-worn point. Shortage or no shortage of sleep; pain; the coma; was the patient dying?

'. . . Was there any evidence of what might be called dreadful suffering or discomfort?'

Dr Ashby [reflectively]: 'Not really of discomfort to such a degree as to render the doctor obliged to give priority to relieving discomfort over the chances of survival.'

One recalls Dr Douthwaite's prompt objections.

The Judge cuts in to ask whether there is really little doubt she could not have survived.

Dr Ashby: 'What I am trying to say is that I, personally, do not think she could have survived the sedation recorded in the nursing books.' [Looking up.] 'And I am certain beyond any shred of doubt that she could not have survived the doses *prescribed.*'

The Judge: 'In your evidence, Dr Ashby, you have assumed that all the drugs prescribed were in fact given?'

'That has heavily influenced me.'

The Attorney-General: 'You recall Nurse Randall telling us that on all his visits the Doctor asked for a glass of hot water? What does this indicate to you?'

'I should say the use of a syringe.'

Could Dr Ashby try to divide the medical history into chapters for the convenience of the jury?

Dr Ashby says he will try to do so. The first chapter began in 1948 with the stroke, the early administration of drugs, and the gradual addiction. The transition to the second chapter was rather vague, but one might say it began some time in the summer of 1950 when the doses had to be raised to satisfy the increased craving for the drugs. If he had been asked advice at that time, he would have pointed out that whereas before it was already extremely important to wean the patient, now it was vital because she had come to a stage of considerable requirement. She was still very irritable, and really he does not think she was getting as much morphia and heroin as she needed. There was a spiral and a dilemma, and a solution had become obligatory, for disaster was the only other result. The third and last chapter began in November. 'I regard it as the time when there was virtually no hope of the patient's recovering from the effects of the previous circumstances.'

And presently, the Attorney-General's last question.

'Can you see any reason why this lady should have died on November 13th if the heroin and morphia had *not* been administered?'

Dr Ashby's answer is hardly conclusive.

'I do not *think* she would have died. I can see no reason in these reports to have expected her to die.' [More assured] 'She was sitting up in her chair quite brightly only a few days before.'

The Crown has finished. There is a sense of being nowhere.

Mr Lawrence, about to go into perhaps the most important cross-examination of the case, begins effortlessly, no strain is showing on the threshold of this unrehearsed and unrepeatable performance.

[*Parlante*] 'You say you do not think she would have died by November 13th if she had not been given the drugs mentioned in the nurses' notebooks?'

Dr Ashby [genial but firm]: 'I do say that.'

Mr Lawrence: 'Is it quite impossible to say that if she had *not* had all the medication recorded through the earlier months, she would *not* have lived as long as November 13th?'

[Smiling gently] 'No, I don't think I agree. I don't think the earlier treatment had any great influence on the length of her life. She *might* have died from natural causes earlier. I accept that fully.'

Mr Lawrence: 'So you are bound to say this: "If she had not had the drugs I cannot be certain she would have lived as long as November 13th"?'

'It depends on what you imply for the reason. The morphia and heroin would have some deleterious effect, though I don't think her life expectation was materially altered by it. But nor do I think it was any protection against sudden death from natural causes.'

Mr Lawrence [silky]: 'Life is so full of chances?'

Dr Ashby nods.

[Still silky] 'There are such gaps in knowledge?'

'Yes.'

[Sheer cream] 'In medical knowledge?' [Return to briskness] 'It is quite impossible to say, isn't it, that if she had not had the medication she would necessarily have lived longer than November 13th?'

Dr Ashby [unshaken, unhurried]: 'It is really a matter of conjecture. There was no obvious cause for her dying, other than a very heavy pressure of drugs and natural causes combining. That is all, I can say no more.'

'There *are* some limits to the power of a doctor?'

Dr Ashby [readily; a little wryly]: 'We are very limited in our powers. Particularly in prophecy about life and death.'

Mr Lawrence: 'That is exactly what I thought. And equally about what causes death?'

'Particularly immediate, or rather, unexpected death.'

'It is equally unsafe to be dogmatic about how long any given person would have lived but for this or but for that?'

Dr Ashby: 'Certainly; and I hope I have not been dogmatic about it.'

Mr Lawrence: 'When you say that the Doctor murdered Mrs Morell, or don't you say that?'

[Touch of good humour] 'I don't think it is for me to say that.' [Temperately] 'I have done my best to guide the court as to what would be the result of certain actions and chemicals; I don't really feel in a position to say that on a certain day or even a certain week the Doctor decided to murder Mrs Morell, I do not feel this is my duty . . .'

'It may not be what you conceive to be your duty, but you *cannot* say that on any day or week he made up his mind to kill her?'

Dr Ashby: 'I certainly cannot say that of any day, but I feel that the instruction to keep her under would have had almost certain effects, and the doses of four and five grains of heroin a day would also have pretty certain effects.' [Pause] 'But I am not prepared to say whether they were instructions of a murderous nature.'

The Judge: 'I think Dr Ashby is quite right to leave out the word murder. But were they instructions of a nature to shorten life?'

The law, these human agents of the law, are very careful. The scales at a capital trial are weighted in favour of the accused, and at the same time there is the literal respect for life itself: the law does not say, this woman was old, this woman was dying, the law does not ask what a life was worth. Ungrudged day after day is spent dispassionately thrashing out whether there has been an intent to kill in one man's mind, whether one woman's span was cut some weeks before its time. In our day, when there co-exist the hideous evils of arbitrary arrest, torture, and set-piece trials. . . . Admirable, indeed. But does it not strike us that our sense is intermittent and our conscience split? Can we not imagine that if our descendants were asked a hundred and fifty years from now what struck them as most shocking and discrepant in our present time, they might point – provided they'll be there to tell the tale – to the hair-splitting niceties of this trial combined with the acceptance of the H-bomb as an example of our staggering schizophrenia.

Dr Ashby: 'Instructions to keep her under would be almost certain to accelerate death.'

The Judge: 'And that is a conclusion a man of the Doctor's qualifications would have reached?'

'Yes, I think an anaesthetist is particularly conversant with the dangers of a patient being unconscious or semi-conscious.'

Mr Lawrence: 'Anaesthesia could be described as an acute poisoning producing unconsciousness?'

Dr Ashby [very nicely]: 'I could have thought of a more flattering description.'

Mr Lawrence: 'In anaesthetics, heroin is not used at all?'

Dr Ashby agrees.

'The anaesthetics in common use in 1950 were still gas and ether?'

'Yes.'

[Concentratedly] 'If we are going to talk about instructions calculated to shorten life, is it not vitally important that we should be accurate about what those instructions are?'

'Yes.'

'And try to find out in what circumstances they were given?'

'Essentially.'

Mr Lawrence: 'I am referring to Nurse Randall's statement, which said, "It was doctor's orders to keep her from getting restless, to keep her under as much as we could at that state." That is *not* the same as instructions to "keep the patient under"?'

'I don't think it is *quite* the same.'

[Pressing] 'It is clear that the object was to avoid restlessness, excitement?'

Dr Ashby [soberly]: 'That is one of the interpretations, and I think it is a fair one. I don't necessarily think that it was that.'

Here some counsel might have left well alone; Mr Lawrence risks carrying it to the limit. 'But it may well be that the drugs after November 8th *were* given with the sole object of promoting her comfort?'

Quietly, not over-enthusiastically, Dr Ashby, the prosecution's expert, gives an answer of immense value to the defence: 'I think that is a possible interpretation.'

Mr Lawrence is coming to 'What may well be the most important single entry in the nursing books, the entry for October 9th, reading, "? stroke".'

Dr Ashby [lucidly]: 'The clinical deductions from this rather slim information are compatible with a certain vascular accident, but I think it is equally compatible with the rather heavy injections at that time – I am not saying that is what happened, but this single entry is explicable on either ground and I would not care to say which is the more likely. . . . '

Mr Lawrence: 'Is it permissible to remember that this is an old woman who has already had one stroke?' Oh, most certainly. 'And in old people like that with an arterial condition, a second cerebral accident of some degree or other is by no means uncommon?' By no means uncommon.

Mr Lawrence [on the spot]: 'It *is* very often the thing that carries them off?'

Dr Ashby [meditatively]: 'Yes – I think they are more likely to die of another stroke than of heart failure.' [Making his decision; clearly] 'Yes, I will accept that.'

Across the road, during the short adjournment:

'No blinking murder. Old girl just died of a stroke. Whatever next?'

'I always say no good comes of these cases with no body.'

'They couldn't help that.'

'Did *you* hear one word about determining an act of murder from the A.G.?'

'It was all good solid overdoses on Day One.'

'Jolly unsporting.'

'Well, it was only what they call opening high.'

'Lawrence *has* got him off this time?'

'As far as that ever goes. Case isn't over yet, you know.'

'Exactly: there's the case for the defence.'

'Oh, it hardly ever works out that way. Defending counsel usually cuts his figure in the other fellow's case. . . . '

'Mr L has had his hour?'

'Never count your verdict until you see the jury coming in.'

'*See?*'

'The way they walk; what they do with their eyes.... If you've seen it once, you *know*.'

'Do they mind so much, convicting?'

'They mind bringing in the bad news.'

'Come on, let's acquire a cross-tolerance to whisky and its chemical ally, gin.'

During the afternoon, some easier passages.

'Did you hear Dr Douthwaite's and the Attorney-General's repeated use of the term maximum dose?'

Dr Ashby: 'I did.'

[Scorn and assurance] 'There is *no such thing* known in the medical profession as the maximum dose in respect to these drugs?'

[Willingly] 'I quite agree.'

Mr Lawrence: 'Let me read you a passage of the 1948 edition of the British Pharmacopoeia. "It must be clearly understood that the doses mentioned in the Pharmacopoeia are not authoritatively enjoined as binding upon prescribers." Do you agree, Dr Ashby, that it is extremely difficult, if not impossible, to talk about fatal doses of opiate drugs?'

'It is.'

'It all applies to an infinite number of individual patients... all different?'

Dr Ashby: 'I'm afraid so.'

'Can you tell us how drugs are tested for maximum doses?'

'We have different batches of animals injected with progressive doses. First none die, then a few, then more; at last, all.'

Mr Lawrence: 'Would you be prepared to accept some well-authenticated examples of the variability of morphia and heroin?'

[Interest on his face] 'I would.'

'The first is a hundred and twenty grains of morphia given by mouth to a patient who was not tolerant and who survived.'

Dr Ashby [captivated]: 'Just out of the blue? That *is* remarkable....'

One would like to know under what circumstances a patient was given a hundred and twenty grains of morphia by mouth. Dr Ashby may ask after hours; we shall never know.

'And another one of twenty grains to a person, not tolerant, who survived. And when you pass from non-tolerant people getting their first dose to people who have acquired tolerance, then it is even more difficult to say what the level of a fatal dose will be?'

Dr Ashby: 'Yes. The absolute maximum dose. But we have a working rule of thumb, some indication can be got from the patient's recorded responses to much smaller doses. . . . '

Mr Lawrence mentions a curious point which has not yet been touched on, though it must have been quite obvious. It is the fact that Mrs Morell cannot have been a *conscious* drug addict. She never realized; she never suspected. How then could she have arrived at that presumed dependence on the Doctor? Mr Lawrence says, 'When she was having these drugs day after day, is there any evidence of craving in the nursing reports?'

Dr Ashby, in full concession, 'There is not.'

'It is clear that she never once asked for an injection?'

[Almost gaily] 'I thought of that one too.'

The Judge suddenly asks, 'Does heroin give that sense of joy – right to the end?'

Dr Ashby: 'We cannot say.'

Presently Mr Lawrence winds up tight again for the last stretch, and the mood is picked up in court.

'Dr Ashby – in October, at the beginning of the spiral, the final increase in drugs, she may *well* have had another stroke?'

During an argument there is an impulse to move up to the opponent, to come close to him. In an English court counsel cannot get near his witness; he stands in his row, the other in his box, between them there is crowded space: and across that, his words, his voice, his will, must seize and hold.

'And the Doctor, coping with the situation, may well have come to the conclusion that there was no more point in a change, in an attempt to wean her, and that he must go on, that death would overtake the spiral?' He would accept that, says Dr Ashby. 'And the case goes on and the Doctor is forced into the spiral until he reaches a point of no return?' Yes. 'And then it is his major preoccupation to promote her comfort and ease distress?' Yes. '*That* is the impasse in which you said yesterday the Doctor and the patient were?' [Sheer will] 'All that I have just been putting to you is a possible view of the case, is it not?'

'A *possible* view. Yes, I think it is.'

'Will you look at the last report of all, the report by the night nurse?' [He reads] ' "Seems a little quieter, appears asleep, respiration 50. 2 a.m., passed away quietly." ' [Low voice] 'On the face of that record, Dr Ashby, is it possible to rule out that when the end came – in that way – at that time – on that day – it was the result of natural causes?'

After a brief pause, Dr Ashby says, 'That cannot be ruled out.' His expression is not to be read.

Mr Lawrence: 'And in those circumstances that entry on the cremation form, "cerebral thrombosis", may very well have been an honest entry?'

Dr Ashby, still inscrutable, 'Yes, I think he could well have thought that was the immediate cause of death.'

For some reason, Mr Lawrence chooses to end *diminuendo*. 'Dr Ashby, you have never been in general practice?'

'That is so.'

'You do not actually see the patient?'

'No.'

'As a consultant, what has been your role?'

Dr Ashby, in a quiet tone, 'I sat in the other chair.'

The Attorney-General: 'Can it be said, in the sense in which the phrase is commonly used and leaving out medical technicalities, that her death was due to natural causes?'

Dr Ashby: 'I do not think she could have survived that dosage of drugs, but that dosage might well have killed her by an apparent natural cause such as thrombosis or terminal pneumonia.'

And this as good as wipes the sense off the answers given to the defence.

The Judge: 'So it may be said that death was the result in the end of natural causes, but those natural causes were themselves the result of the drugs given by the Doctor?'

Dr Ashby: 'Certainly.'

'And that, looked at in the ordinary common-sense way, means that the cause of death was the result of the drugs given by the Doctor?'

'Yes.'

The Judge: '*Now* I think you *have* said that in your view that was the cause of death?'

But Dr Ashby will not stay pinned down. 'I should make it clear, with great respect – I can only say it in this way – I don't think it is absolutely possible to rule out a sudden catastrophic intervention by natural causes, just as it is not possible to say that this woman did not have another cerebral haemorrhage, say, at one o'clock in the morning. . . . It is not possible to rule it out.'

As he steps down, nobody can be wholly pleased; nor can anybody be really vexed with Dr Ashby, his honesty was too patent. His was no hedging; here was a man clear-minded enough, conscientious enough, come to think of it: brave enough, to refrain from tidying up the ambiguities of fact.

DAY THIRTEEN

MR LAWRENCE is expected to open this morning with his first speech to the jury, the first sustained, explicit opportunity of the defence. After a few minutes with a formal and belated witness, the case for the prosecution rests. Mr Lawrence turns to the Judge and *sotto voce* asks leave to proceed without the jury. The Judge expresses the opinion that he does not like the jury to be absent from a case. Mr Lawrence hesitates, bows, gathers himself, and, facing the bench, begins.

'My Lord – I wish to make a submission in law. My submission is that on review of the whole of the evidence produced by the Crown no sufficient evidence to support the indictment has been disclosed. There is no justification for allowing this case to go any further. . . .'

It is no less than a plea of No case to answer. If it were successful, that is, accepted by the Judge, the case would have to stop then and there, the prisoner be discharged, the jury dismissed. . . . There have been rumours enough that the defence would try this bid; now it comes as something of a shock: it is like hearing a man call, *Banco*. The whole move has a curiously unrealistic air; it is not that there may not be strong grounds for Mr Lawrence's submission, it is simply too much – it is felt that to throw out the case at this point is just not thinkable.

As Mr Lawrence speaks, the Judge sits composed in patience. There is no suspense – although Mr Lawrence is heard with interest and appreciation – and one might almost swear that he himself is not aware of this. His delivery is fluent, lucidly paced, and he speaks without notes.

He keeps it up for two whole hours.

His argument runs as follows. The burden of proof in a case of this sort never shifts, the burden of making out a charge of murder is always upon the Crown. What has to be disclosed by the prosecution is a real case and not 'some shabby adumbration of bare possibility'. His client is charged with the murder of Mrs Morell, and that involves the Crown in producing a case on at least two essential matters – first, that by some act or acts of the accused her death was in fact brought about, and secondly, that that act was the reflection of a deliberate intent to bring about her death. He submits that on neither of these two essential matters has a case of sufficient strength to go to the jury been made out.

This is a case based exclusively on medical evidence. Without medical evidence there would not be any case at all. And on this evidence, the field of inquiry must be narrowed to a period of a few days. Although disapproval of the medication has been expressed by the doctors, nothing has been put forward by either of them to suggest that before November 1950 that medication was in any way devised with the deliberate purpose of bringing about her death. Dr Douthwaite committed himself that the intention to kill was formed on October 31st, and this excludes from his view the formation of any such intent before that date. Thus, it is inescapable that the field of inquiry is narrowed to the final period of the life of Mrs Morell, and during that final period she was a dying woman. Which brings one to the point which really lies at the threshold of this inquiry, which is: whether any case has been made out that this lady's death was in fact the result of an act of murder. The prosecution say that this was a death caused by the administration of drugs. They are committed to adequate proof of the interlinking of cause and effect in that respect. 'It is no answer to say that these are all very difficult matters and that causation – what caused this and what caused that – is a matter of speculation which may land you in realms outside these courts altogether; this is a criminal charge, and this man should not be put in peril of the gravest charge in the criminal calendar unless there is adequate evidence upon that matter.' Once it is conceded as a *possibility*, not a fantastic possibility, but a reasonable medical possibility, that the death when it came was not the result of the drugs she had had in any sense at all, then the matter is at large and it is impossible for any reasonably minded jury to find that the matter had been proved to their satisfaction.

This is the main line, and as soon as it has been developed, Mr Lawrence hurries on as if forestalling interruption.

'I think that without going to any extreme length we can interpret what Dr Ashby said as this, "I think the morphia and heroin given were the cause of death; but that is only my view and I cannot exclude the possibility that it was nothing of the sort and that when her death came it came as a result of an intervention." It is significant that Dr Ashby used the word "intervention" which can only mean the operation of some external and independent force intervening in a situation; and what Dr Ashby is really saying is this, "I can't rule out the medical possibility that the actual death was not linked by cause and effect with the drugging but was due to sudden intervention by some natural cause." '

(What Mr Lawrence is saying here is in effect, 'A. whips out a revolver, aims it at B., and is about to pull the trigger when the ceiling comes down and kills B. B. is killed by an intervention.' But has this altered the original situation, or affected the intention?)

'. . . It is a case where on the prosecution's own evidence the matter is poised equivocally and uncertainly. This is only another way of saying that the evidence is inadequate.'

'Mr Lawrence,' the Judge interposes mildly, 'you have considered, have you not, Dr Douthwaite's evidence? The jury will have to consider whether they prefer the evidence of Dr Douthwaite or Dr Ashby.'

Mr Lawrence: 'My Lord, I would submit, not. Dr Ashby is not a doctor called for the defence, but for the Crown as a part of the Crown's case.' [Very energetically] 'If you have one doctor say one thing and another doctor on the same side say another, it shows that there is no reasonable certainty about it, it draws attention to the weakness of the case. That is how I would put it.'

He draws a breath and goes on like a man from another country.

'In any case, I do not desire your Lordship to think that this is the most important point I am making. I submit quite boldly: if there was any sort of case on the medical aspect of this matter for me to answer by the time Dr Ashby went into the box, by the time Dr Ashby had left the box that case, whatever it was, had completely disappeared because Dr Ashby not only did not find himself forced to postulate murder, but he conceded that there was a reasonable possible alternative view, and that it might well be that the drugs were administered with an entirely innocent intent.'

The Judge [and it *is* an interruption]: 'What this will lead to, Mr Lawrence, is this, is it not, that Dr Ashby in the end conceded it, you may say, a reasonable possible alternative view that the Doctor was caught up in a situation which he solved wrongly, it may be, but quite innocently?'

[Eagerly] 'Yes, my Lord, and that is clear beyond any shadow of doubt later on – '

The Judge [sitting back]: 'Your submission contains two points which to me seem to present difficulty. It might be said of Dr Douthwaite's evidence, looked at as a whole, that he conceded your alternative possible view; and it might be said that he did not. The point is that it is not for me to take that determination out of the hands of the jury. The second difficulty is this:' [talking voice] '*supposing* that we can take the evidence of Dr Douthwaite and Dr Ashby to be something like this, "We know the treatment was wrong, we think a doctor with his qualifications ought to have known that it was wrong, but we concede as an alternative that he might not have known", if the evidence rested there, then it might be said that I should have to direct the jury that it was not strong enough; but if one finds that a doctor has in fact benefited by death, and that he thought or knew he would benefit by death, and that the drugs administered by this doctor who benefited were (if that is the right medical view) wrong and unnecessary and caused the death – do not these three factors put together call for an explanation by the Doctor?'

Mr Lawrence: 'With the greatest respect, my Lord, that is not the way the evidence stands at this stage. The prosecution cannot have it both ways. Both doctors say that there was what Dr Ashby called a point of no return, both doctors mean by that the moment when her death was inevitable whatever anybody did, and it is central to their evidence that there was no felonious intention before the time of that point of no return. So if they are right that it was wrong treatment but innocent treatment, then the Doctor cannot be criticized in terms of murder for the fact that the irreversible condition was reached on or about November 8th.' [Suddenly rhetorical] 'I find in the case for the prosecution that measure of doubt, that measure of uncertainty, that measure of lack of strength . . . ' [then rapidly] 'I am now coming to the police evidence – '

The Judge [no mistaking short shrift this time]: 'Mr Lawrence, my conclusion is that the two doctors' evidence does give rise to questions which can only be properly determined by the jury.'

It is dismissal. Mr Lawrence stands as if lost. There is an immediate resumption of rustling. The Judge, in his other voice, adds a few words to say that it is not desirable that he should comment at this stage. The Doctor – it is one of the moments when one looks at him – sits if anything more contained. Then the court adjourns quickly, a little before the usual time. Presently, a junior taps Mr Lawrence on the shoulder, and he gives a start.

'Now why did he have to do that?'

'In these things a miss is as bad as a mile.'

'*Not* if the jury had been sent out.'

'As requested!'

'It was a loss from the moment the Judge decided to keep the jury in.'

'Well, Lawrence's words were not designed to go straight to *their* hearts.'

'Hardly hearts.'

'Waste of audience endurance.'

'It was put very well, didn't you think? A treat in its way.'

'Oh, the performance was not at fault; only the place.'

'They heard the Judge say No. This jury listens to this Judge.'

'There was his chance to put it all to them in his own sweet way and no one to say him boo till the end of his case; and what does he do, puts himself in the position to be contradicted, *and* turned down, *in front of them* before the morning's out.'

'He should have dropped it when he heard the jury were going to stay in. Why didn't he?'

'Why didn't he? Why does anybody in this case behave the way he does?'

The defence have something else to put across this afternoon. The Judge is hardly in his chair when Mr Lawrence says unobtrusively that having talked all morning he does not think it necessary to open with a speech to the jury at this stage. The Judge nods, Mr Lawrence gabbles on, innocent and businesslike, 'My first witness will be Dr John Bishop Harman and I think I should tell your Lordship that the defence have decided in the circumstances of this case not to call the Doctor.'

The first brute reaction to this is the, relative, disturbance of a dozen and a half reporters stumbling over benches and each other to run the news to a telephone. Mr Lawrence, with firm matter-of-factness, drives on the case.

'Dr Harman?'

'Physician?'

'Consulting physician at St Thomas's Hospital?'

'You have had experience in the treatment of cerebral thrombosis in elderly people?'

Mr Lawrence is heard for the first time in the part of examiner-in-chief. Up to him now to show the witness to his best advantage.

'You have experienced many such cases?' Dr Harman has. 'You are familiar with the problems arising in the treatment?' Dr Harman is. 'Are you able to deduce the nature and degree of Mrs Morell's illness at that time?'

Dr Harman is dark, well-built, and fluent. As medical expert for the defence, he might be said to be the man who chose to step into the lions' den, though this could not be deduced from his demeanour. No one in the box since the police witnesses has found himself so soon at home.

'I think it was clear she had had quite a severe stroke and was paralysed.' [Breezy] 'There was further, I think, a rather difficult mental condition.'

Mr Lawrence: 'I will begin at the beginning. You have seen the Cheshire reports? Are you prepared to condemn or not to condemn the use of morphia during her stay in Cheshire?'

'I am certainly not prepared to condemn.' The answer comes a shade too quickly.

Mr Lawrence: 'And what do you say about the introduction of heroin later on by the Doctor?'

[Crisply] 'I should say it was unusual. ... It is not a drug commonly given.'

'What is the usual reason for it?'

'Pain.'

'And what is the effect?'

'Compared with morphia there is less soporific action.'

'Do you see anything sinister in its introduction?'

'*Nothing at all* sinister.' Carefree rather than olympian or dogmatic, the witness has his own brand of certainty.

Mr Lawrence [wholly second violin]: 'Looking at the nursing notes up to the spring of 1950, what do you say is a fair summary of the position?'

Dr Harman [trenchant and urbane]: 'I should say she had recovered from her stroke as far as she is ever going to; that she's reached a stage at which one might describe her as being partially crippled, but there are no signs of anything further about to happen.'

Mr Lawrence: 'What do you say about the continued medication at that period of the regular doses, day after day, of a quarter grain of morphia and a third of heroin?'

[Lively] 'The clearest thing about that is, that by that time it had been going on for a year and some months. . . . It would certainly have to be continued even if it was producing no good. I can see no evidence it was producing any harm.'

Mr Lawrence: 'Why do you say it would have to be continued?'

'Because she was by then addicted.'

'In what sense do you mean addicted?'

'I mean one would have had to continue with what she was having in order to prevent her from getting withdrawal symptoms; in other words,' [factual and elated] 'a clear-cut illness lasting about ten days which, while not exactly dangerous, would be extremely unpleasant.'

Mr Lawrence: 'If that had been envisaged, would she have had to have some substitute drug?'

'Well, I think that sort of patient, in that sort of state, certainly would. If the Doctor had withdrawn, he would only have done it with a view to starting again later since he thought morphia and heroin useful drugs for her.' [Gently] 'I can see the need for withdrawal from a young or middle-aged person with a normal life before them, but in this case the patient was crippled and was going to remain crippled. . . . '

Mr Lawrence: 'So far as heroin is concerned, have you ever

known of its use in cases other than severe pain?' The Attorney-General's question.

Dr Harman [airily]: 'Oh yes, I've used it in such cases.'

'The nurses say that Mrs Morell was bad tempered, irritable, and given to outbursts?'

'Then I think it extremely likely that these drugs would have been helpful.'

Mr Lawrence: 'Ordinarily speaking, would you expect them to make an existing irritability better or worse?'

'It would be rash to say exactly what any of these drugs would do in a different patient.' [With ease] 'The test is what they do do. Ordinarily they are given to *reduce* irritability, and in the majority of cases they succeed.'

'When the Doctor was away on holiday, his partner stepped up the morphia by the introduction of Omnopon. What does that indicate to you, Dr Harman?'

'Presumably the patient was getting restless and needed more sedative.'

'Was it or was it not reasonable for the partner to do that?'

[Promptly] 'Entirely reasonable.'

Mr Lawrence [referring to the nursing book entry '? stroke']: 'What about that possibility?'

Dr Harman [full self-possession]: 'There are several points to consider. There was a significant increase in the dosage, she had difficulty in speech. . . . Semi-consciousness can equally well be produced by drugs or by a stroke.'

'Supposing it was a stroke, what would you expect from a patient of that age and history?'

[With abandon] 'If it was a stroke, I should expect further trouble leading progressively to deterioration and unless something else intervened to natural death from old age.'

As simple as that. Has the Doctor just nodded his head? The Doctor sits unbudged. But the Doctor is now discounted. He will not be called. . . . Not called to speak, to explain, not called to stand for the answer. The explosive was a dud, the oracle has renounced its voice, the fountain will stay in the sand. . . . From now on, the issue is a technical one, not innocence or guilt but a matter of reasonable doubt, of links in the chain of evidence, of a case made out or not, of law. The plausible, the probable truth, not the absolute. . . . We shall not know what was in this man's heart.

It is his good right of course, right human and in law, that goes without saying. Or does it? The prosecution cannot comment on the chosen silence of an accused; a judge may; as far as the overt acts and words of men can go, there will be a fair trial. But men also think and feel, juries have a consciousness – they even have, perish the thought, a subconscious and a superconscious – and none of these are amenable to the rules of evidence. 'You must dismiss this, exclude that, leave aside anything you may have heard outside this court. . . . ' Are such injunctions practicable? Minds, vibrating to prejudice and experience, form their own response, are their own law; and it would be a dull mind indeed that does not ask its daily why.

It may well be, this elected silence, a move from strength, counsel inspired, imposed. Economy. Why do more, expose more, explain more, than you must. (A mercurial temperament unreined?) If to speak out may be relief, it is also an ordeal, grinding in these circumstances: cross-examination, the audience's greed, inevitable mulling over shabby detail. . . . Many an accused had cooked his own goose in the witness-box. Why not leave well alone, if well it is – this strange ramshackleness of the prosecution case – why take a risk? Why not stand back? A cool decision.

Why then this sagging feeling, of dust and ashes, this letdown as though the case were done and dead? Is it curiosity cheated? It is. Yet this curiosity, as we call it, is it not one of man's oldest, deepest longings? the desire to hear the tale, to know the truth and meaning, the solution and the cause? The wanting to see the wheels go round, the little boy and the watch, man and his maker, the need for pattern and design: only connect. And with it there is that other longing for what the pattern seen, the design revealed should be – must be! that longing, too, is as young as hope – the desire for symmetry, sense, and justice, the absolute and the answer. The machinery of law, such as we have evolved it, is perhaps a tribute to civilized restraint and melancholy realism; it is not always wholly to the taste of our instincts.

Of course nobody was fool enough to expect the Doctor to talk with the tongues of angels from the witness-box. The answer-to-question convention would soon have put a stop to that. What one did expect – hope again – was that the Doctor felt, and the defence, he could afford to try; try to put across the way it was, try to tell: it was like this and like this and you must believe me because I know, it was me, I was there.

'Let us get on to November. Are you able to take the view similar to the other doctors that she was clearly a dying woman by then?'

Dr Harman: 'I agree roughly. On November 9th it was much more obvious than on November 1st. It is a question of how soon you make your diagnosis. It is clear that at this point the drugs were no longer working.' [Animated] 'This is one of the disadvantages of morphia that at some point later on when one really wants to use it, one finds it is no longer working. That is what I think happened here.'

Mr Lawrence [seizing the opening; earnestly]: 'And do you, or do you not, agree with Dr Ashby that after this point of no return the first duty of a doctor is to promote the comfort of a patient?'

'I do agree.'

'Do you see anything to suggest that these drugs were given with any other object than to promote her comfort?'

Dr Harman [incisively]: 'My own conclusion is that they were given to stop her getting excited, to keep her peaceful, and that they were not working very effectively.'

'Dr Harman, I want to ask you about the dosage of paraldehyde?'

[Big] 'I should not *think* of giving as little as 5 c.c. in a case like this. . . . I never give less than 6 c.c.'

'Is it a safe hypnotic?'

'The safest! Even if she had had that other injection of 5 c.c. on top of the earlier 5 c.c., it would still have been within the normal limits. It was not a large dose.'

'On the evidence of the nurses' reports, was it a morphia death or not?'

Dr Harman goes into the symptoms. The commonest form of morphia death, is death in a coma from respiratory paralysis, when respiration becomes more and more slow, as slow as 10 or 6 times a minute. The few times when respiration rates are mentioned in the nurses' notes the figure is 50, which is very high. Nor does he interpret 'appears asleep; passed away quietly' as a morphia coma. That is merely his interpretation; she was certainly unconscious. He has also considered the jerkiness and twitchings mentioned by the nurses; there is little known about morphia convulsions and when at first he thought the twitchings might be that, he looked up reports. He has gone through world medical literature, covering more than ten thousand separate references, and he found descriptions of only eighteen morphia convulsions, most of them referring to Chinese coolies, and extremely sketchy. . . . When Nurse Randall was in the witness-box and tried to describe the convulsions, did Mr Lawrence recall how she had unconsciously jerked her forearm the way she must have seen the arm of Mrs Morell move?

(This is imaginative and true, one does see Nurse Randall's arm flicking up and down from the elbow as she stood protesting about the twitchings she had seen.)

'Whereas in a morphia convulsion, *all* muscles and particularly the strong muscles in the back go into a slow, tense spasm; the subject is jerked violently backwards, the head snaps back, the palms are thrust out, the mouth is drawn down, the eyes start out of the head, the face goes black. A person would be talking normally as I am now, then suddenly go like this – ' With no further warning Dr Harman proceeds to turn into a Madame-Tussaud sight.

When one looks again it is still going on – spluttering and shaking, slowly, slowly, Dr Harman is doubling himself over backwards in the witness-box. Seconds pass. The Judge does not move a muscle.

Dr Harman is straightened up again. 'And then a person comes back like that. . . . ' He pats down his hair.

Mr Lawrence looks as though he might be about to say, Thank you, Dr Harman. Then everything goes on.

'What do you say then about the death of this patient?'

Dr Harman [easily, though not without a touch of wry compassion]: 'I should say that in old ladies over eighty who have had strokes and arterio-sclerosis, one does not regard it as a question so much of explaining the cause of death. One knows they just die.' [Shrug] 'It is very difficult to know for certain why they die.'

Mr Lawrence: 'The immediate terminal cause might well be due to some catastrophe – ? A clot in the heart, for instance?'

'That can be a very usual thing.'

[Insisting] 'Is there any necessity then to link that death, from a cause and effect point of view, with any of the drugs that have gone before?'

Dr Harman: 'I see no necessity to link her death with the doses administered.' Like Dr Douthwaite, he is very certain.

Mr Lawrence: 'Is it possible it could be so linked?'

[Dismissing] 'Oh, it is possible, yes.'

'Could you say whether one hypothesis is more likely than another?'

[Breezy] 'One might say there was rather a large dose of hypnotics . . . and that in general is a bad thing.' [Decided] 'But there is no evidence for it one way or the other.'

Mr Lawrence: 'What about the dosages of these drugs such as they were recorded? What do you say about those? Are they within the general experience of practitioners?'

'In my view, certainly! Not in all practitioners' experience, but in some – a reasonable number – a few times in their life.'

Mr Lawrence: 'Have you yourself encountered cases where this amount has been given?'

'Oh, yes, I've had comparable cases; I should not have regarded this as anything to talk about to friends when talking medical shop.'

There stirs the kind of resistance that had been engendered before by the prosecution's unusually large syringe. In court one develops a sixth sense about a witness and his evidence, and it can be quite strong; the trouble is that it may also be mistaken.

Mr Lawrence: 'Would you have expected the doses to have a fatal result on Mrs Morell?'

Dr Harman: '*My* comment is that I would not expect anything. I cannot say that death would not occur.' [Pause] 'It might very well. But what I would not say is that it *would* have occurred.' [Positive] 'Morphia and heroin are drugs outstanding in their variability of effect. I made researches into histories of addicts in hospitals. . . . The highest daily morphia injection I could discover was 77 grains every day, and the highest dose of heroin 40 grains.'

Mr Lawrence [neutral, prompting]: 'If it be suggested that cases of that sort are freak cases, let me ask you if the doses recorded in the nurses' books are of the freak kind or not?'

'Not freak at all!' [Hearty] 'That would not be the sort of dosage one would even talk to a colleague as something worth talking about. . . . '

(A few days ago Dr Douthwaite had said in this same box that the doses were colossal.)

Mr Lawrence: 'Can anybody say with any degree of accuracy or truth that this or that amount would be fatal to any patient?'

Dr Harman [ready for it]: 'Not to any degree of accuracy or truth.'

('Why can't they have a medical assessor on the bench who'd tell them one way or the other?'

'A board of assessors.'

'Appointed by whom? Acting for whom?'

'The Home Office? The Crown?'

'The Ministry of Health.'

'A jury outside the jury?'

'Nobody's infallible. . . . '

'It wouldn't wash.'

'Not in this country.'

'It'd wash better than this. . . . ')

'It has been suggested that the Doctor as an anaesthetist would know more about the long-term effect of morphia and heroin?'

Dr Harman [waxing more abandoned]: 'I can see no importance in that at all. I know a good many anaesthetists who don't.'

[Titters.]

Mr Lawrence [sweeping on]: 'One of the other doctors has said that the alternative to morphia and heroin in the last stages should have been hyoscine.' What is Dr Harman's view of that?

He must confess he did not even consider hyoscine. He was surprised to hear it was suggested. He would not have recommended it. It is now a general rule that morphia and heroin are not used pre-operatively in patients over sixty.

Mr Lawrence: 'The Doctor did not turn to hyoscine but to paraldehyde. Can you think of anything better or safer that he could have turned to?'

Dr Harman [happily]: 'That is exactly what I would have done.'

The day is over. There is a hollow feeling that the defence is taking it a bit too easy. Dr Harman, perhaps, does not protest enough.

DAY FOURTEEN

MR LAWRENCE has not done with Dr Harman and Dr Harman is soon again in his stride.

Has he ever used morphia and heroin together on a patient?

He has; but generally sees little point in using them both as their actions are so similar. He certainly doesn't regard it as dangerous, that has never been his opinion; indeed, he has never heard it expressed before. Oh, it is a fair opinion, when all is said and done, on a rather marginal question.

Does he recollect, asks Mr Lawrence, that Dr Douthwaite told this court it was axiomatic that heroin should not be given to people over seventy?

There is no reason at all, says Dr Harman, why heroin should not be given to elderly people.

'Do you agree with Dr Douthwaite that to instruct nurses to give heroin s.o.s. was an astonishing suggestion?'

'I was not astonished at all. A nurse would know what I wanted, and be capable of detecting the symptoms. I frequently give such instructions myself.'

Dr Harman's last answer is still ringing in our ears when the Attorney-General opens with the assault direct.

'Dr Harman, have you ever practised as a general practitioner?'

'Only a fortnight.'

'Prior to this case, have you had any occasion to make any special study of heroin and morphia?'

'No special study.'

'You are a recognized authority on a disease known as Q fever?'

'I have described cases.'

'And is Dr Douthwaite a recognized authority on heroin and morphia?'

'He is.'

The Attorney-General has turned formidable. His questions,

rolled up sluggishly like so much thunder, are delivered with a crushing weight of condemnation, and this stolid exhalation of disapproval is as damaging as the use of detailed cleverness.

'It is very important you should not shut your eyes to the obvious, or not give certain factors their full weight?'

'It is.'

'Do doctors normally prescribe morphia and heroin without the intention of using them on the patient?'

'I should think not.'

'You have seen the summary of the prescriptions? And you have seen that for the last five days the Doctor prescribed 41 grains of morphia and 39 grains of heroin?'

'Yes.'

'Did you ignore these factors before expressing an opinion?'

'No.'

'Assuming that all those drugs so prescribed were administered to Mrs Morell during the five days, what, in your opinion, would the effect have been?'

Dr Harman: 'I should be very unwilling to suggest what the effect would have been.'

[Measured toll] 'I am asking for your opinion.'

[Noticeably determined to stick it out] 'She certainly could have survived those doses.'

'*Of that quantity?*'

'I think it is possible.'

'Do you think it is *likely*?'

Dr Harman: 'Yes, I think it is likely.'

The Attorney-General: 'Would you have expected these doses to do her any good?'

[Cocky] 'They might have done.'

The Attorney-General: 'If she had those prescriptions given her in that short period, *that* would have formed a topic of medical shop?'

'Yes, those doses would.'

'Have you ever heard of any doses like that being prescribed to a dying old lady of eighty-one?'

Dr Harman: 'I have not heard of an exactly comparable case.'

'*You* would never prescribe doses of that quantity for a lady of that age?'

'I have never prescribed them.'

'And you *would* never?'

Dr Harman: 'I am not prepared to say what I would do.'

The Attorney-General [thudding]: 'Do you think you would ever prescribe doses of that magnitude?'

[*Contre-cœur*] 'I do not think I would.'

'Have you ever heard of any doses like that being prescribed for a lady of eighty-one?'

'Yes.'

'A dying lady, not dying of an inoperable disease?'

'The lady I was thinking of was not dying at all.'

[Pleased with his uptake] 'But this lady, according to you, was?'

'Yes.'

'Did you hear Dr Douthwaite's evidence that in his opinion each one of these prescriptions on these days was a lethal dose?'

[Not too happily] 'I don't agree with that opinion.'

The Attorney-General: '*You* disagree with Dr Douthwaite?'

'I do.'

'Dr Harman, most of the views you have expressed here about drugs, were they formed after reading books before this case?'

'Yes.' [Pause] 'That is one of the usual ways of gaining knowledge.'

'How many drug addicts have you treated?'

'Two or three. One was a heroin addict and the others morphia.'

'One heroin addict is not a very representative experience on which to base a general opinion? How long ago was that?'

'It was just before the war.'

The Attorney-General: 'Your answers to my learned friend yesterday possibly conveyed a different impression of the range of your experience? That impression conveyed to his Lordship and the jury would be an erroneous impression?'

Dr Harman: 'I don't think so.'

'Your dramatic acting yesterday afternoon was based, was it not, on what you read of that kind of convulsions?'

'Yes.'

'You have never seen a morphia convulsion?'

'No.'

[Whipping out a tome] 'Have you ever heard of . . . [it sounds like Thomas] – ?'

Dr Harman says he has not.

'The greatest authority on drug addiction?'

'There are many authorities, not any one necessarily the greatest.'

Presently, the Attorney-General asks if Dr Harman knows of any reason why no attempt had been made to wean Mrs Morell?

'She seems to have been getting on very well and the attempt wasn't necessarily worth it.'

'*You* have never made this attempt?'

'No.'

'If weaning causes discomfort to a rich patient, it might mean the loss of the rich patient?'

'It might.'

Is it proper treatment to keep a person who has had a stroke drugged?

He would say it was quite usual.

'Have you ever done it?'

'Yes.'

'Have you treated *many* patients with a stroke?'

'I have.'

[Very nasty] 'Hundreds?'

[Very nasty] '*Hundreds.*'

'Have you ever kept a patient who had a stroke under drugs for two years?'

'Not for two years, not under heroin and morphia.'

'What is the longest you have ever kept someone who has had a stroke under heroin and morphia?'

'I do not normally use them for a patient with a stroke.'

The Attorney-General [quick swoop]: 'That would be bad for the patient's health?'

'Not necessarily!'

'Is it *good* for the patient's health to be a drug addict?'

Dr Harman: 'No.'

'Let us be quite frank, Doctor: prolonged drugging does have a deleterious effect on a patient's general health?'

'It depends what you mean by drugging.'

[Declamatory] 'Routine injections of the character described in the nursing notes. Routine injections of morphia and heroin.' [Lower gear] 'Would these be beneficial to health?'

They might be; they might be neutral and they might be deleterious. . . . It depends on how they are used. He cannot see anything that suggests this drugging was deleterious.

The Attorney-General [rising note]: 'I am asking you, as a consultant, if you were told that a lady in her late seventies had this course of medication over two years, would you have expected that to be good for her general health?'

Dr Harman: 'I should inquire into the circumstances before I expressed an opinion.'

'And having inquired?'

'It would depend on what the circumstances were.'

The Attorney-General turns away. 'Well, if you do not want to answer, I will not press you.'

When the court resumes after luncheon, the jury-box is empty. There has been throughout a certain anxiety lest one or the other of the jurors should fall ill or in some way fail to turn up one fine morning. A trial can carry on with eleven, even with ten, but not with less. The Judge comes in. Still no jury. Mr Lawrence gets on his feet and imparts in funereal accents that it is his duty to bring to my Lord's attention a publication which he understands has been bought this morning in the London area. A magazine is handed to the usher who presents it to the dais. The Judge takes it with two fingers, holds it up by an end as if it were a dead rat, then puts it down and spends some time peering at it.

'My Lord, with respect, I have marked the relevant page. . . .'

'Ah, yes. . . .'

Silence.

The Judge: 'It calls itself – ' [reading as though with some difficulty] ' "The magazine of news significance" . . . '

(On the back benches, questions form. Everyone feels absurdly guilty. *Time?* Other lips shape the syllables, *Newsweek.*)

The Attorney-General now comes in on it. 'My Lord – I want to say – My learned friend has warned me of this er . . . publication during the short adjournment. . . . I have ordered an investigation.'

The Judge, Mr Lawrence, and the Attorney-General face each other in consternation.

('I've got it. In my pocket. I guess if someone on the jury does, this trial's had it.')

It must be hampering to have to thrash this out in front of an audience of eighty avid Press-men.

'It would, in my submission, be unwise . . . '

'Any reference to this prejudicial material . . . '

'In the circumstances, with respect . . . '

The consensus is, least said soonest mended. The jury is sent for. When they are back, probably the more curious for their waiting, the Judge addresses them in sorrow. His attention has been drawn to a publication. . . . It is not, he is glad to say, one of the newspapers of the daily Press with whose names we are all familiar. He is not going to name it. It contains some undesirable comment on the proceedings that are taking place in this court. He would propose that in order that there might be no possible suggestion that such material has entered their heads, they should be careful not to buy any newspapers other than the ordinary newspapers. The fact is, he thinks, that the rules which British justice requires to be observed in these matters may not be so well known to those who are responsible for the Press in other countries. He does not know, and that is why he is asking them to leave journalistic material other than the well-known daily Press out of their reading. And he would take this opportunity of reminding them again not to discuss any aspects of this case with anyone. This trial, certainly, has gone on longer than he expected when it began. . . .

That is all, and they are left to make as much of it or as little as they choose. All questions are left unspoken. The Attorney-General proceeds at once to cross-examine Dr Harman about paraldehyde.

'Do you say' [all stops out] 'you never give less than 6 c.c. of paraldehyde?'

Dr Harman: 'In disturbed persons, yes.'

'Have you ever given 6 c.c. to a woman of eighty-one?'

'I'm not quite sure. I should not have counted it anything to remember if I had.'

'Was I wrong in gaining the impression from you yesterday that anything less than 6 c.c. was quite safe?'

Dr Harman: 'What I wanted to convey was that anything less than 6 c.c. in these circumstances was unlikely to do any good.'

There was a difference, was there not, between administering paraldehyde to someone who has had no previous history of hypnotic medication, and administering it to a woman who is almost saturated with morphia and heroin?

There was a difference.

The Attorney-General [with his full weight]: 'Are you saying as a doctor, and a consultant, that you can express the positive opinion that these administrations of paraldehyde, if they took place, had nothing to do with her death?'

'Yes, I would, in so far as one can express an opinion on the evidence.'

The Attorney-General [making it very difficult to stick to it]: 'Do you really say then that the paraldehyde administered that night by the Doctor and subsequently by Nurse Randall could in your opinion have had no effect upon her death?'

Dr Harman: 'I do.'

When a doctor gives medical evidence at a trial, the eyes of the profession are upon him; and, although God knows that the profession does not appear united in their views, an expert witness is hardly able to postulate something entirely wild.

'If she *had* been given the prescribed 12 grains of heroin on November 12th – what would have been the result?'

Dr Harman: 'I would not predict.'

The Attorney-General: '*You really think she could have survived at that time 12 grains of heroin on top of the paraldehyde?*'

'From what I know of morphia and heroin I shouldn't have been surprised if she had.'

'You do not really know very much, do you?'

Dr Harman: 'No, and that is why I am just surprised.'

[Heavily] 'Are you saying, as a consultant at St Thomas's, that in your opinion heroin and morphia neither caused nor contributed to her death directly or indirectly?'

'Yes, I am saying that. I said that yesterday, and that is still my opinion.' He adds, 'Most of her symptoms were symptoms of her illness and not of medication.'

The Attorney-General [fullest boom]: 'It is your considered opinion that she could have survived the doses prescribed to her by the Doctor?'

'That is my opinion, yes.'

A pause; and then the last shot. 'Did you obtain any information from the Doctor for the purpose of forming your opinion?'

And Dr Harman's answer to that is a firm, unqualified 'No.'

Mr Lawrence enters the breach and makes a few skilful points on medical fallibility. The court hears of some more freak doses. The highest is one of 577 grains of morphia to a woman. The woman died.

The Judge: 'Dr Harman, there is a phrase I should like to make clear so that there may be no dispute about the exact nature of the meaning.' The phrase, accelerating death. Does it mean a real cutting short of life, though not necessarily for a sinister purpose? Does Dr Harman agree or not that the instructions 'to keep under' would accelerate death?

Dr Harman says, no, he does not think that.

Does he attach any significance at all to that instruction during the last thirteen days?

Yes; it signifies to him that the patient had got now to the stage of delirium in which she would have remained distressed, excited, and uncontrollable if she had not been under some influence of drugs.

The Judge: 'Therefore in your view they were the right and natural instructions to give?'

'I would go further and say that sort of policy, if it was a policy, is quite common in such cases.'

The Judge asks him to recollect Dr Ashby's answer that the instructions to keep under would have been almost certain to accelerate death.

Dr Harman: 'I would put the emphasis the other way round, I would agree that it might have done so; but I should say that it would more probably have not.'

The Judge says that will be all. The defence calls a Miss Mildred Vickary who gives formal evidence about the Cheshire Hospital nursing notes; there is no cross-examination; and this, we understand, will be the end of the defence witnesses. No friend of the Doctor's, no friend of Mrs Morell's, no member of their households or their families is going to be called. Dr Turner, who had charge of Mrs Morell in Cheshire and who was to have given medical evidence, has had, it is announced, a heart attack three days ago.

'You believe Dr Harman is right?'
'I don't know.'
'You believe Dr Douthwaite was?'
'I don't think so.'
'Do you believe Dr Ashby?'
'Yes. But I don't know what he said.'
'Then what do you believe?'
'Dr Ashby.'
'But what did he *say*?'
'I don't know.'

DAY FIFTEEN

'TODAY is the fifteenth day of this trial and for the first time – and it will be for the last time – I rise to address you on behalf of the accused – '

It has gone on so long; now it is racing to an end. . . . There will be no more questions; the facts, such as they are, have been heard. What remains is the putting of the facts – tidied, arranged, intelligible – before the jury by three agents in three patterns. The closing speeches: the speech for the defence; the speech for the Crown; the Judge's summing-up.

Mr Lawrence speaks from his usual place in counsel's row, standing slight and alert. This time he *is* addressing the jury.

'In all those fifteen days, there has been one word of six letters, one word' [he makes it very slow, very solemn, very hushed] 'which should, but not always has dominated the proceedings.' [Whisper] 'That is the word murder.'

There is not, one feels, the fullest response. It may be that we have lived too daily with that concept; or that Mr Lawrence's greatest strength lies not perhaps in commanding emotion. There is, of course, rigid silence.

' . . . Of all the murder cases that have been heard in this famous court, surely this is one of the most extraordinary. Let us remember right at the outset what the Doctor is accused of. It is this: that he deliberately murdered an old woman who was his patient at a time when she was already dying and had no more than possibly a very few days or weeks to live.' [Very intelligibly and down to earth] 'Is that not a most extraordinary case that a doctor should be accused of murdering one of his patients when she was dying already? With no intervention on his part the end was inevitable. And *that* is the case alleged against him.

' . . . The burden of proof lies on the prosecution. And that means that possibility of guilt is not enough – suspicion is not enough – probability is not enough – likelihood is not enough. It is certainty beyond a reasonable doubt that is required!'

. . . Justice here is the paramount consideration, and the only way in which justice can be done is by judging the matter on what has been heard in this court, and in this court alone. [*Brio moderato*] 'What you read in the papers, what you hear in the train, what you hear in the cafés and restaurants, what your friends and relations come and tell you, rumour, gossip, all the rest of it, may be so wrong. . . .

'. . . The prosecution has taken thirteen days to present its case;' [hard] 'the defence has taken one day and a half. It is time this case was shortened and brought to an end. . . .

'There is another matter on which I want to say something to you.' [In sorrow] 'You may very well have been wondering why the Doctor did not go into the witness-box. The Doctor, and all the other people who have stood in the dock on other charges, are never bound to go into the witness-box; indeed, it was only at the beginning of this century that the law even allowed them to do it.'

There is a faint stir.

'. . . The burden resting upon counsel defending a man accused of murder is a very grave and heavy burden. We stand here as the Doctor's shield at all the stages of the case; and there is no more grave moment of anxiety than when the question arises, shall the accused go into the witness-box? Looking at the case as it stood after the days when I had, perhaps wearisomely, cross-examined the witnesses, you may think that there was nothing left of it, nothing substantial for the Doctor to meet, and it is not our duty – and you would not want us to – to put the Doctor in the box for the entertainment of the spectators in this court or for the edification of the Press. Can you begin to understand the strain under which this professional man has been living for the last four or five months, in prison day after day, night after night, awaiting his trial?' [Swelling tone] 'Then a fortnight or more of sitting silent through the long hours in this court when witness after witness gave evidence, and at the end of that, would you expect or want him to go into the witness-box and endure the ordeal of question on question by me, to say nothing of cross-examination by the Attorney-General, unless it was absolutely necessary to do so?'

They must remember that all these matters relating to Mrs Morell happened six years ago. [Very fluent] 'Mr Sogno, the solicitor, remembered nothing about it except what he could recollect from his notes. *He* had got notes. The nurses have had their notes put to them (with results we all remember).... When the policemen gave their evidence, there was not one of them that went into the box who did not have notes on the desk in front of him. The Doctor has no notes. At the end of all this unbearable strain, the Doctor would have been asked to cast back his memory over the gulf of six years,' [declamatory] 'and at every stage there would have been the terrible realization that one failure of recollection, one inaccuracy, however innocent, would be seized on and might well be put before you as an indication of guilt....'

[*Vibrato*] 'But surely the greatest justification for the decision in this most extraordinary case is that by the mercy of heaven there has been provided for you, members of the jury, one witness that is both eloquent and unchallengeable – that is the witness in these paper notebooks made by the nurses day after day, month after month, when their memory was as fresh as paint....'

And now down to the case itself.

Cheshire, June 1948, the stroke. Mrs Morell – ill, old, paralysed, autocratic, difficult, and a very wealthy woman.... The first morphia given in Cheshire, 'a great signpost'. The medical outlook – six to twelve months to live.

'What was she to do during this time?'

And what could the Doctor do? Make her life as bearable as possible, give her sleep at night and make her cooperative with the nurses, for otherwise the irritability, the outbursts and brainstorms would exhaust her. He put her on a régime of morphia and heroin, with tablets for pain. 'What the prosecution are doing, via Dr Douthwaite, is to launch an attack on the use of heroin.' That is not the issue in this case. 'You are not judging whether the Doctor was a good doctor or not. There are good doctors, better doctors, and there are not so good doctors, but all are honest men doing their best according to their individual skill.' What they do may not commend itself always to the grand ones at the top of the profession, but that doesn't mean that they are murderers. . . .

The picture from now to the summer of 1950 is that of an old lady, getting about in the car, sitting out in the garden, being helped because she could not walk without help . . . 'You may well think that the Doctor was doing his duty to the best of his ability and not doing it too badly. And he was doing it on a regular régime of these drugs. . . .

'It has been said that this was wrong because she became addicted. . . . ' But to an old lady who, the doctors thought, had no more than six to twelve months to live, paralysed, given to brain trouble and outbursts, what does a little dependence on a drug matter? If she had been weaned, she could not have gone on without some other sort of sedation, so what was the point?

'In September Dr Harris appeared on the scene and found the situation was getting worse. . . . ' To cope with it, he increased the morphia. . . .

And now her last fortnight, the *vital fortnight* in November. 'What do you see is happening?' The old woman dying, the restlessness getting worse. . . . We talk of restlessness, but when that restlessness originates from an irreparable injury to the brain it may be as distressing, both to the patient and to those who have to look after her, as pain. 'Who is to judge between these things? Is a doctor to say, "Well, you have got a very severe pain and I am therefore entitled to relieve your misery with drugs"? But if the doctor sees an old woman in the last days of her life, restless, wakeful, distressed, miserable, is he to say, "Oh, no, you lie there; if you toss, if you complain, if you do irrational things, if you exhaust yourself, if your life is generally wretched and miserable, I am not going to help you"? . . .

'What was in the Doctor's mind when he gave Mrs Morell these drugs?' Was it an intent to kill, or was it an intent to do the best he could, with his – perhaps rather limited – knowledge as a general practitioner, to ease the misery of this dying woman?

In those last days there were given ten separate doses of atropine. It has as far as we know some kind of antidotal effect on morphia. 'Do you think a murderer intending by dose after dose to bring about her death, who comes each morning and says, "Good heavens, she isn't dead yet, give her another one," do you think for a moment that a man like that would have taken the trouble and interest to ease a symptom like mucus by giving atropine? It doesn't make sense, does it?

'... On the evening of November 12th it is getting clear that the morphia and heroin are not giving this woman any sleep and peace. So what does this diabolical murderer do? he chooses the safest drug in the market, he turns to paraldehyde, an old-fashioned, well-established hypnotic. ... I apologize to you for building up this point – it does not need building up.'

'Members of the jury, what is left?' Dr Douthwaite's theory. 'On any view of the matter, Dr Douthwaite's theory is rather strange. It was quite an extraordinary performance in an expert witness called for the Crown in the course of a murder charge. I am not imputing any lack of faith to Dr Douthwaite, but I am submitting to you it was a very strange performance. And I put it before you that the whole way in which it was done was an indication of the uncertainty there must be about these matters. Dr Douthwaite came here prepared to give evidence upon the situation as it was before the nurses' notebooks came into the case. When, at a rather dramatic moment – of which this trial has had too many – the Attorney-General asked Dr Douthwaite what was his conclusion, he answered, "I am driven to the conclusion that the Doctor formed the intent to murder on November 8th." Two days later, after Dr Douthwaite had stood for many more hours answering questions in this court, he told the Judge for the first time that he had a theory on the Doctor's withdrawal of morphia on November 1st. ... The situation was so strange that my Lord offered me the opportunity of further cross-examination.'

As for the theory of the accumulation of morphia in the body, the whole thing breaks down, doesn't it, because it has been dissented from by two doctors, Dr Ashby and Dr Harman. 'And when you have two eminent medical men disagreeing with the whole theory, and if Dr Douthwaite's theory of accumulation in the body is wrong as a scientific fact, then the whole theory of murder comes collapsing to the ground.'

'Members of the jury, where are you?' This is not a morphia death. ... The doses prescribed during these last days are well within the average doses currently prescribed. ... 'Is it not likely' [gently] 'that nature intervened and said the time has come, and at that moment something happened as it happens to all of us at the close of our lives? As Dr Harman said, "People just die" ...' And if she died from natural causes, she did not die of drugs; and if she did not die of drugs, the Doctor did not kill her, and if he did not kill her, he is not a murderer. ...

A slight pause. Then resuming with great energy.

'What I submit is one of the most significant features here is the behaviour of those nurses, trained women. As the case was closed, and the last entry was made in the books, they did not have the slightest suspicion that it wasn't one of the usual unhappy endings to a case, just another case – They go off duty and the matter is ended for six years. ...'

(Actually, neither side ever touched upon that point. The nurses were not asked.)

[Lively] 'Members of the jury, what is left?' A murder for gain. ... 'Let us have the facts of this once more. There is no evidence at all that the Doctor was short of money. The gross value of Mrs Morell's estate turns out to be £175,000. Her chauffeur got £1,000. Nurse Randall got £300. All sorts of people got legacies of £500 and £1,000. But this murderous doctor gets the absolute bequest of some silver in a cupboard the value of which is £275!

'The other gift in that will, a car, a pre-war Rolls-Royce, was a gift dependent upon the son to die before his mother. The utterly fantastic hypothesis is put before you that this doctor when he has got a dying woman as a patient – whose life is limited to a term of hours or days or weeks – for the sake of getting a bit of silver in a cabinet, for the sake of getting a Rolls-Royce which he couldn't get anyhow because the son is still alive (I don't know whether the prosecution are suggesting he ought to have killed the son first?), that this doctor, instead of standing back and letting nature take its course, suddenly embarks upon a course of murder. It is too ludicrous! And yet it is *solemnly* suggested that he had a motive. ...'

... About the cremation certificate. Members of the jury –

something said to a police officer – late – in the dark – The Doctor didn't remember then *when* he knew, or didn't know, that the stuff did not come to him under the will – He couldn't remember suddenly on that night, in the street, six years later, what the state of his knowledge was when he filled in that form –

What else? The police evidence. That curious episode in the surgery when the Doctor is supposed to have stated that he gave nearly all the drugs prescribed to Mrs Morell. . . . Even if he had in fact stated this, his recollection must have been *absolutely wrong* because the records show that most of the injections were given by the nurses; the jury has only to look at the notebooks to see that the Doctor did not give all the injections. . . . [With forceful common sense] 'The point is not what the Doctor prescribed in circumstances which no one could forecast with accuracy, but what was administered, and the evidence for that is in the notebooks.

' "Easing the passing of a dying person is not all that wicked. She wanted to die. That can't be murder. It is impossible to accuse a doctor." Let us not fall into confusion about this. There is a world of difference between giving drugs which shorten life, and giving merciful administration to ease the passing – not to hasten it – but to give quiet at the end. . . . "*Murder, murder,* can you prove it was *murder*? She was dying in any event." These are not the confessions of a guilty man!' [Great strength] 'They are the incredulous reactions of an innocent man who was absolutely stunned by the monstrosity of the charge brought against him in his professional capacity. Trying to ease the last hours of the dying is a doctor's duty and it has been turned and twisted into an accusation for murder. . . .'

And after three hours and a half, the wind-up, the last words.

'Members of the jury – I do not suppose you will ever forget that for three weeks out of your lives you were called to sit in judgement. . . . Let it not be a memory that will haunt your conscience. . . . When I have finished, my voice will be silent for the rest of this case.' [Calm, firm, slightly *decrescendo*] 'If you think, as I submit, there should be no conviction, be steadfast in that belief to the end, be steadfast and so reach a true verdict. . . .'

There can be no applause; no sign. The Attorney-General rises without delay. Steadfastness is put at once to the test.

The Attorney-General begins by pointing out that his voice, too, is heard now for the last time. '... Without the artifice of advocacy – we also have a duty, we for the Crown – We have a duty, too – You, members of the jury, have listened very patiently through the long days – You will come to your conclusions from the evidence you have heard in this court, from the documents you have seen proved – ' [Solemn boom] 'No one wants to see an innocent man convicted on a charge such as this, but, on that evidence, members of the jury, as reasonable men and women of the world, you may find it proved – as in my submission it is proved – that Mrs Morell was killed by the deliberate act of the accused, a criminal who has killed for profit behind what he thought the safety of the sacred patient-doctor relationship.'

... What was done in a nursing home in Cheshire is wholly irrelevant and throws no light on subsequent events. As she had morphia there, it was not unreasonable to continue it for a little.

'For a *little* ... ' Our first main question is why, from July 1948 on, morphia and heroin together were prescribed? 'Even Dr Harman could not suggest an answer to that, Dr Harman who nearly fell over in the witness-box in his demonstration, who nearly fell over backwards in his efforts to help the defence ...

'You have heard his answers – were they not evasive? Was there not an absence of frankness? And were not some of them wholly incredible? In my submission, Dr Harman was an unsatisfactory witness.'

... Too much must not be made of the Doctor's old-fashioned qualifications. Why should it be assumed that he had not kept himself up to date, or that a man holding a post as anaesthetist should not know about the newer things in drugs? It should not be forgotten that the Doctor told Superintendent Hannam in relation to morphia and heroin that he 'very very seldom used them'. Why was she made a drug addict by the Doctor? Might an explanation not be that the springs of gratitude were more likely to be opened if this rich old lady found that in spite of her stroke she was feeling daily remarkably well owing to the injections given her by the Doctor, injections of heroin, which produces as one of its main characteristics that feeling of well-being? Might not the Doctor's object have been to make this rich lady well disposed towards him with a view of benefiting under her will?

It is a faithful echo of the opening speech, with little added or forgotten.

He must now speak of the nurses' notebooks. 'The prosecution submits that they are true as far as they go, but they do not reveal the whole truth.' ... A special injection was an injection of which the nurses did not know the ingredients; it is not to be assumed that all those special injections were always the same.... According to Nurse Randall, the one thing the Doctor wanted on all his visits was a glass of hot water, in Dr Ashby's evidence that was indicative of the use of a syringe. ... Is there not a very significant and important difference between the doses recorded on the books and the prescriptions? 'And where did those notebooks come from?' The nurses told us they were usually destroyed after the patient had died. These had been kept. 'Who kept them? From 1950 to 1957? Who had an interest in keeping them? There was *only one person*: the Doctor.

'We know that the Doctor kept no records. May he not have thought that at some time or other some inquiry such as we are now engaged in might arise?' If the Doctor formed a design for murder, would he not take the greatest care to secure that any entries made by the nurses were not obviously incriminating to him? Would he not try to arrange things so that the entries in the books would not look too bad? [Ominous roll] 'Why were those books kept till 1957 when all the Doctor's other records were destroyed?'

And now the time is up and the court rises and adjourns for the week-end. The prosecution speech is interrupted for three days; the Doctor vanishes through the floor, to the prison van that will take him to the prison cell in a suburb of London where he will wait once more from a Friday to a Monday, three evenings, three nights, and two full days, sixty-six hours.

THE LAST WEEK

THE SUMMING-UP

DAY SIXTEEN

TODAY (the Attorney-General is presumed to cease speaking some time in the morning) is the day of the Judge's summing-up. The court is packed as it was on Day One.

The Crown resumes at once.

'*We* know that the legal effect of tearing up a codicil revoking a bequest is nil, *we* know that it does not revive the bequest. We know that, but did the Doctor know it? Let us see what the position was before Mrs Morell's death. She was a drug addict as a result of his treatment. She executes a will under which he is to benefit; perhaps not as much as he hoped. If he knew about the codicil, he may have thought there was quite a chance he would get less. By securing her death, he may have thought that he was making sure of getting at least what she had left him. . . .'

. . . ' "Murder? Murder? Can you *prove* it was murder – " As I said to you when opening the case, is that what you would have expected an innocent man to say? Is it, as my learned friend suggested, the incredulous reaction of a man falsely accused? Or was it the sort of statement a shaken man might have made, a shaken man who had committed murder which he thought could not be proved? What he said was, "Can you PROVE it was murder? I don't think you CAN PROVE murder – she was dying in any event." '

. . . It was quite natural when Dr Harris took over for a short period that he should have followed the instructions given by the Doctor. No significance should be attached to the fact that he carried on the course of medication or added a little Omnopon. . . .
'I suggest to you that the reason Mrs Morell was so angry with the Doctor for going away on holiday was that he had been giving her additional quantities of drugs without the nurses knowing and

Dr Harris carried on with only what the nurses had been giving her.'

It is a shrewd point, but there is no evidence for it.

'The Doctor comes flying back from Scotland not on account of her illness but to look after his own interests. . . .'

. . . He is coming now to the really vital period of this case – 31 October, the day when instructions were given to omit the morphia and the Omnopon. Why was that done? Would one not normally expect that the stopping of the main sedative meant that the patient was getting better and did not need it any more, not that she was getting worse? This action had puzzled Dr Douthwaite. . . . It led him to conclude that the intention was to terminate life. Dr Douthwaite did not use the word murder himself. 'You saw Dr Douthwaite in the witness-box, a senior physician at Guy's Hospital and a recognized authority on heroin and morphia. You would expect any doctor to do his utmost to find an innocent explanation before expressing the view that the object was that of securing the death of the patient. Dr Douthwaite's evidence, tested as it was by long cross-examination, never changed as to the cause of death. . . . Dr Ashby said that she could not have survived the pressure of sedation during the last four days; Dr Douthwaite said that the dosages could only result in death. Dr Harman agreed that the policy was to give her an injection whenever she woke up. Why was it done? In the Crown's submission there is only one conclusion. . . .'

. . . The court has heard about the jerky spasms on the last night. Both Dr Douthwaite and Dr Ashby expressed the opinion that these spasms were due to heroin. Dr Harman tried to establish that the nursing entries must refer to something else. 'There can be no doubt really that the convulsions of which she suffered were due to the large doses of heroin. Yet the defence invites you to come to the conclusion that she died of natural causes! It is asserted that it is not proved that she did not die a natural death!'

. . . He supposes that in any murder case it can be said that the victim does not die immediately, that although he was shot, stabbed, or poisoned, it wasn't the shooting, stabbing, or poisoning which led to his death, but that he might have died of natural causes in spite of the injury inflicted on him. 'I suppose it may be said that if you see a man walking on the railway line run down by a train he might have had a heart attack as the train struck him and so died of natural causes and not of being hit by the train. But in this case, on the evidence of the treatment,' [full tones] 'of the large doses of heroin and morphia given in the last days, of the terrible jerky spasms leading up to the evening of her death, of the injections of paraldehyde just before her death, in this case to ignore that evidence and to say death was due to natural causes would be to ignore the obvious!' [Pause] 'In my submission, it is proved beyond all reasonable doubt that the cause of the death of Mrs Morell was the administration of these drugs, and that her death was due to the morphia and the heroin, and accelerated by paraldehyde. Members of the jury, murder in this case has been proved. It is for those reasons that I submit to you that the proper verdict in this case is one of murder.'

*

Before the Judge begins to speak, there is a final clearing, a wave of settling back, then there is perfect silence. The wigs and papers in the well have come to rest; in counsel's row the black and white figures sit with arms folded inside their sleeves. The Judge makes his turn, leans slightly forward, and begins. The voice from the robed public form is private, though immensely practised; the words are spoken words, nearly intimate and at the same time quite aloof.

The jury never take their eyes off him.

'You' [looking at them] 'are the sole judges of fact, and from your verdict on a matter of fact there is no appeal. *My* task is to tell you the law. My task in this case is a light one; there is very little question of law that is in dispute. I propose to deal first with the law, then with certain irrelevancies and inessentials in this case, and then go through the events chronologically.'

There goes a breath as of assuagement through the ranks.

'There are four matters of law of which I must tell you. The first is what is meant in law by the word murder. Murder is an act, or a series of acts, which were intended to kill and did, in fact, kill. *It does not matter for this purpose if death was inevitable.* If life was cut short by weeks or months it is just as much murder as if it were cut short by years. . . .

'There has been a good deal of discussion about the circumstances in which a doctor might be justified in giving drugs which would shorten life in cases of severe pain. It is my duty to tell you that the law knows no special defence of this character. But' [a movement of hands] 'that does not mean that a doctor aiding the sick or the dying has to calculate in minutes or hours, or perhaps in days or weeks, the effect on a patient's life of the medicines which he administers. If the first purpose of medicine – the restoration of health – can no longer be achieved, there is still much for the doctor to do, and he is entitled to do all that is proper and necessary to relieve pain and suffering even if the measures he takes may incidentally shorten life.' Manifestly there must be cases in hospitals day after day in which a doctor is faced by whether a certain treatment prolongs or shortens life by hours and perhaps even longer. The doctor who decides to administer or not to administer is of course not thinking in terms of hours and minutes of life; he could not do his job properly if he were. 'If, for example, a doctor had done something or omitted to do something and death occurs, say, on the 11th or 12th or on the Monday instead of the Tuesday, no one with common sense would say the doctor caused the death. They would say the cause of death was the injury or whatever it was that brought her to hospital. But it remains a fact, and remains a law, that no doctor has the right to cut off life deliberately. I say it to you so that there can be no mistake.' No defence of this kind has been put forward in this case, or in any other case. 'What counsel for the defence was saying, was that the treatment that was given by the Doctor was designed to promote comfort; and if it was the right and proper treatment of the case, the fact that incidentally it shortened life does not give any grounds for convicting him of murder.'

'The second matter of law is that it is for me to say whether there is evidence on any particular point, and not allow you to be troubled with the point unless there is some evidence. . . .'

And this leads to the swift disposal of one of the most troubling questions in the case:

[Quite trenchant] 'I do, therefore, direct you as a matter of law that there is no evidence on which you could properly come to the conclusion that any drugs were administered to Mrs Morell over and above the injections recorded in the nurses' notebooks. If the case for the prosecution had rested solely on the prescription list and the suggestion that the quantities shown there had been administered to Mrs Morell, I should not have allowed the case to go to you at all.'

This could be taken for an *amende honorable* for the brusque dismissal of Mr Lawrence's submission.

The third matter of law concerns the fact that the jury must necessarily have heard a good deal about the Doctor, and perhaps remember what they may have read about him in the Press. 'I should like to say this, and I say it with the approval of the Lord Chief Justice – it is not desirable that on matters of this sort judges should express what are merely their personal views – I think it would have been wiser in this case if the preliminary proceedings before the magistrates had been held in private. Because when you have a case which arouses widespread discussion it is inevitable that reports should appear in the Press which are read by the public and consequently by members of the public who might be asked to serve on the jury; and the proceedings before the preliminary magistrates were quite different from the proceedings as they emerged in this court. . . .

'But having said that, members of the jury, I venture to wonder whether, after three weeks of sitting in this court, there is anything left of it that really affects your mind. If you have not learned within those weeks to distinguish between what is solid fact, sifted, gone over again and again, and what is gossip and rumour, then, members of the jury, you will not be the sort of jury that I believe you are and that ordinarily serves in these courts. If you have not learned to distinguish as easily as one can distinguish, if one is an expert, between different textures of stuff – good quality, on the one hand, and shoddy, on the other – between what is evidence and really proves something, and what is mere suspicion, gossip, and of no value whatsoever, then, as I say, you would have learned nothing. But I am completely confident that you have, and I entertain no doubt at all that anything that may conceivably have been in your minds at the beginning has sunk to the bottom, as it were, as the dregs which will trouble you not at all in arriving at your verdict.'

A man speaking seated from a dais makes a different impact, and uses a different manner from a man speaking standing from the floor. Unlike counsel, who gets up every time he wants to say a single word, a judge never stands. Yet the chair on the bench is no arm-chair.

The fourth and final matter of law is that the burden of proof is on the prosecution. '... It is their duty to satisfy you beyond reasonable doubt before you arrive at a verdict of guilty. The accused, as he sits in the dock, is as innocent as anyone else in the court, and will so remain until the jury by their verdict have convicted him. The Doctor sitting there has the right to the advantage' [in his easy voice] 'of what I may call the initial incredulity that any assertion of that sort, that a doctor has murdered his patient, would give rise to in the minds of ordinary men. And the prosecution must demolish that....

'Reasonable doubt does not mean a feverish or haunting doubt, a doubt which one might wake up with in the middle of the night. It means a cool, sane, reasonable doubt....

'... The rule that you must be satisfied beyond all reasonable doubt is a rule which is expressly designed for the benefit of the accused. Satisfaction on the balance of probabilities is not enough. That means, does it not, that persons who may probably be criminals, but cannot be shown to be so beyond a reasonable doubt, go free. You may feel if you started to speculate about it, that that is not a state of affairs that you like to see. You may feel you ought to be allowed to consider all the material that might seem to you to be relevant and not to be restricted to what is put before you in this court. But, members of the jury, whether you like the rules or not, they are the rules which you must accept and must be bound by. *Anything outside the evidence is outside your responsibility*, and your responsibility, Heaven knows, is great enough. It is not your responsibility to wonder what might happen if you allow a man to go free who is probably a criminal. The rule about reasonable doubt is the instrument which is given to you to use, and you are not responsible for whether it is the right or wrong instrument, it is the one that you must use. . . . These rules are not inventions that have not been found to work. They are rules which have been well settled by generations of experience. They are rules, I think, which accord with our notions of how justice should be administered. They are not lawyers' rules. We pride ourselves, do we not, that a man who is convicted by a jury is undoubtedly guilty. The price of making sure that the innocent are not convicted must be that the guilty sometimes go free. It is to carry out that great principle that the common law has evolved these rules, the rules of evidence and proof, and it is upon those rules that our juries have been instructed for generations. . . .'

'. . . Anything outside the evidence in this court is outside your responsibility.' . . . What is not evidence is what they might think the Doctor might have said or not have said if he had gone into the witness-box. But where they have a rather more difficult and unusual task is where there is a conflict between two opinions, opinions given by experts, in this case medical men. 'In most cases medical evidence is only ancillary and plays a minor part, whereas in this case the prosecution has had to rely upon their medical evidence to establish the very fact of murder. And there you have three eminent physicians going into the witness-box and disagreeing with each other. . . . You have heard the examinations and cross-examinations and got a general impression from them. . . .' But the jury are not a board of medical assessors who can decide between the doctor witnesses on the basis of which is medically the more correct; they are not in a position to give them so many marks for each answer. . . . They have to deal with it in the sort of way they might find themselves having to deal with conflicting medical opinion in the ordinary course of their lives. Suppose, for example, someone dear to them – one of their family or a relative – was a patient and they called in doctors, and having called in all the best doctors they get conflicting opinions, as one may do; in the end they would have to make up their mind as to which was the more likely to be right. 'And fundamentally your task in this court is just that: you will have to make up your mind. What impression did the doctors make upon you in the witness-box? Which of them inspired the most confidence? You saw them and you listened to them. You heard their qualifications. You heard the answers they gave. You have heard their answers criticized. You have heard Dr Harman criticized by the Attorney-General. You have heard Dr Douthwaite criticized by Mr Lawrence, not on the basis, as I understand it, that he is not a great authority, but much more on the basis that he is a man who jumps to conclusions, who, perhaps naturally without the full material at his disposal, forms an opinion from which he is reluctant to depart. Some people are more opinionated than others. Some people alter their opinions more easily than others. All those things you have to take into account....'

Not all of this, unfortunately, is at all easy to hear. The Judge speaks to the jury at a conversation pitch suitable no doubt for a large room. During the last weeks there had been something on the dais which looked like a microphone; this microphone – if it was that – has been mysteriously removed this morning.

'Another unusual feature – I think it is fair to call it unusual – is that the accused himself has not gone into the witness-box. I say it is unusual, but then in many respects this is an unusual case.... I want to face this frankly with you because it is something that may be troubling your minds. It is perhaps a natural reaction for laymen, and perhaps for lawyers too, to say, "Why hasn't he gone into the witness-box if he is an innocent man? He is the doctor who attended the patient. He can tell us more about this than anyone else can. Why has he not gone into the witness-box, unless he fears that questions will be put to him that he cannot satisfactorily answer?" You heard Mr Lawrence address you on this point. You heard him tell the reasons, or some of the reasons at any rate, why on his advice – and a client might well be a foolish man if he did not in such a matter follow his lawyer's advice – the Doctor had not gone into the witness-box. You may have found those reasons convincing, or you may have not. I am not going to deal with them. What I am going to tell you is simply this – that it does not matter. You have not got to judge whether the reasons are convincing or not. The Doctor has a right not to go in the witness-box. ... I shall elaborate on that at the end because it is so important.... Let me tell you that it would be, in my judgement – and indeed as a matter of Law – utterly wrong if you were to regard the Doctor's silence as contributing in any way towards proof of guilt. The prisoner who goes into the witness-box goes there for his own benefit and his own defence. It is perfectly true that they sometimes make matters worse for themselves. But the prosecution has no right to rely on that at all. The duty of the prosecution is to prove their case before the question ever arises as to whether the prisoner should be called or not. . . .'

But there is another aspect of the matter. The Doctor is also inevitably what might be called a 'potential witness for the defence'. So if the jury finds a gap in the evidence which he might have filled, the gap remains. They are not to speculate, either in his favour or against it, upon what he might have said. 'Let me illustrate this in relation to some of the issues in this case. You heard the police officers give evidence about statements that have been made by the Doctor; you have also heard it suggested that the Doctor had not said some of the things attributed to him. Now you might have said to yourselves, "Well, we see no reason why we shouldn't accept the police evidence provisionally, but of course we must keep open minds until we have the Doctor's version." Well, you have not heard it, and you will not hear it. You are left to decide that question without the potential evidence of the defence. . . . You are not obliged to think that if the Doctor had gone into the witness-box he might have given a convincing answer. . . .'

*

During the short adjournment it is learned that the Doctor's solicitor collapsed in the solicitors' room in the Old Bailey and was taken to a hospital. He, also, has had a heart attack.

'Is he going to finish today?'

'Not enough time.'

'Can't we sit longer? It shouldn't take him more than another three hours or four?'

'It's the jury; he wouldn't like the jury to sit up half the night; or longer.'

'Couldn't he finish up today and have the jury come back and do their stuff tomorrow? Lord, they've been home every damn night since this started. . . .'

'Not after summing-up they can't. They've got to stay where they are till they have their verdict.'

'And after half a summing-up they can go home or any place they please?'

'After nine-tenths. As long as a couple of words are missing.'

'Who fixes it, the time schedule?'

'He does.'

'Well, he should know. But brother, *another* night.'

*

At 2 p.m. the Judge says he will now run as rapidly as he can over the salient dates. It started with the 25th of June, 1948, when Mrs Morell had her stroke. She was up in Cheshire staying with her son, and she went into the hospital where she was given a quarter-grain of morphia per day during the nine days she remained there. 'That has been criticized by Dr Douthwaite, but not by the other doctors in the case.' On 5 July she was moved to Eastbourne by ambulance and the Doctor took charge of her. On 9 July there was the first prescription of morphia. On 21 July heroin was introduced. And that was criticized both by Dr Douthwaite and by Dr Ashby. 'Dr Harman has defended that treatment, but you may think – and it is a matter entirely for you – that he was not altogether enthusiastic about it.'

. . . On 12 February 1949 Nurse Randall came, and therefore remained the night nurse in the case up till Mrs Morell's death.

[Occasionally glancing at a note] ' . . . In the following April there took place the first of two conversations between the Doctor and Mrs Morell's solicitor. It is the first suggestion we have that testamentary matters were under discussion, the first suggestion that the Doctor had got this lady under his influence. . . .

' . . . On the 24th of August the will was made which tells us precisely what the Doctor got. He knew that Mrs Morell, who left an estate of £157,000 net, left most of it to her son, and left a number of legacies that you were reminded of. . . . So you may think that it was not a very great achievement – an oak chest of silver valued at £276, compared with £300 to the night nurse and £1,000 to the chauffeur. . . .'

... In June 1949 the nursing records began. A quarter of a grain of morphia and a quarter of a grain of heroin were given per day; and that, with slight alterations one way or the other, went on for a considerable period right up to the late summer of 1950. ... By September she had seven weeks to live, and that marked the beginning of the change in dosage and the end of what Dr Ashby has called the first of the three medical chapters. It was the period when the level dosage was ending and the spiral dosage was beginning. It was increasing rapidly to such an extent that in Dr Ashby's view it was bound to lead to disaster unless she was weaned. The other factor to note about this time was the opinion of the doctors who studied the reports, and the opinion of the nurses themselves, that she was beginning to go downhill. 'And that' [making a slight pause] 'was an important consideration.'

... In September she executed a codicil cutting the Doctor out of her will. In October, she tore up this codicil and her son posted the pieces to her solicitor. There can be no doubt that it was her intention to replace the Doctor and give him back the legacies from which she had cut him out because he went to Scotland. 'Whether the Doctor knew he was getting any of these things, we do not know.'

... On 9 October she had what may have been another stroke, which the prosecution says was due to the large injections of drugs. ...

... From 31 October there was a marked change in the medication. Morphia was dropped altogether and heroin was continued alone. It was then that Dr Douthwaite diagnosed, or inferred, the Doctor's intent to kill. The new medication went on until 6 November, when the instructions were changed and morphia was reintroduced. Therefore these are crucial dates to bear in mind. ... On the 8th, hyperduric morphia was used; and on the evening of the 9th, instructions were left by the Doctor for one grain of heroin to be given as needed. ... This is about the time when the instructions were given that have been labelled as 'keeping under'.

... On 10 November Dr Ashby begins – again the date is not certain or precise – what he called the third medical chapter. On the morning of that day the Doctor changed instructions from one grain heroin s.o.s., to one grain heroin *hourly* s.o.s. Dr Douthwaite selects that date as marking the complete inevitability of death.

. . . On 12 November, at about 5 o'clock in the afternoon, there is the last recorded injection of morphia and heroin. Later in the evening came the first injection of paraldehyde, and at 2 a.m. of the 13th she died.

. . . The following day the Doctor filled in the cremation form on which he stated he had no pecuniary interest 'in so far as I am aware'; and on the 15th the cremation took place.

. . . In January 1951, the will was proved, and on 6 February the chest of silver was delivered to the Doctor; and at some date about that time the Rolls-Royce was delivered as well.

'Well, then, members of the jury, there is a long gap of some six years, and it is right that you should be reminded, as Mr Lawrence reminded you, that at the end there was no suspicion at all about the way in which Mrs Morell died. The nurses departed and went about their avocations. The estate was cleared up. The relatives dealt with the legacies and other matters, and there was no suggestion that anything sinister had occurred. It is not, in fact, until August or September, the summer of 1956, five and a half years later, that anything is heard of this matter. Then we know that inquiries were made from the nurses by Superintendent Hannam, and they made statements upon which no doubt these proceedings in due course were founded.

'Those inquiries led to four police interviews with the Doctor in 1956. October 1st was the encounter outside the garage which was a casual encounter. . . . The second took place on November 24th when the house was searched for dangerous drugs. There was a conversation about the drugs, the list was given to the Doctor to consider, he made his remark about very very seldom using morphia and heroin. He said all the drugs on the list were used, and he said, "Poor soul, she was in terrible agony."

'The third of the interviews was on the 26th of November at the police station, and then it was that the Doctor referred to easing her passing, and her being a dying woman.

'The last was when the Doctor was arrested on December 19th, and said, "*Murder?* Can you prove it was MURDER?" There was also the phrase to the receptionist. "See you in Heaven." There was a lot of cross-examination on that at the time, but it has disappeared from the case, and quite rightly so. You have not been reminded of it by either side. You cannot attach weight or importance to words of that sort which were obviously said under great emotional strain. . . .'

It is a little late in the day. Those words have been bandied about three continents for the last four months. The importance that can be attached to words said under great emotional strain is another question and perhaps a matter for the psychologists who have been so manifestly absent from this case.

That concludes the review of the dates and facts. . . . 'Let me now deal with some of the matters which I suggest are inessential, inessential in the sense that they do not really help you, or help you very little, to a just determination of the really crucial matters in this case.

'First of all, you have heard, particularly at some of the earlier stages of this case, a good deal of criticism of police action. . . . In this case, and indeed in most cases, police officers have interviews with the accused, and in the ordinary way of things they cannot possibly get down everything that the accused says – Superintendent Hannam said that the Doctor was a loquacious man – and therefore a jury in court has to rely on the sense of fairness of the police to give a fair summary of the conversations and not to twist phrases that were used. That is why it is always relevant to consider the conduct of the police. . . . Therefore I ought to deal shortly with the criticisms that have been made. Perhaps I may say, for what it is worth, it is my opinion as one who has sat here and heard this criticism made many times, that I have seen nothing at all in the conduct of the Scotland Yard officers that appears to me as unfair or oppressive. . . . It is said in the first place that Superintendent Hannam waylaid, a matter which he much denied, the Doctor on the first occasion in order to have this conversation with him, a contrived interview, so to speak. Members of the jury, it would not shock me in the least if he did waylay him. The police have among their duties the waylaying of suspected criminals. If they waylay the right criminal, everybody is very pleased with them. If they waylay the wrong man – and in this case it is for you to determine whether that happened or not – it does not seem to me of itself to be a reasonable criticism of their conduct. It is also said that when Superintendent Hannam went with the search warrant, he was not the man named in the warrant but nevertheless he went there, and it is suggested that he went for the purpose of sending Inspector Pugh out of the room so that he could have an interview with the accused. We are not trying an action for trespass. No doubt it is very important from the constitutional point of view that only the officer who is authorized under the search warrant should be allowed to enter the premises, but you are only considering here what is unfair and oppressive, and it is for you to say whether you think there is anything unfair and oppressive in an interview which is contrived, if you like, with a suspected criminal in order that he may be asked about a prescription list. There are very stringent rules about questioning people in the Doctor's position, and it is not suggested in any way that the police infringed those.

'Then you had the incident of the superintendent's notebook, and I was not in the least shocked by that either. The fact is that it is recognized as common practice and very sensible that when two police officers are both present at an interview, they sit down together afterwards and compare their recollections and decide as far as they can what the exact words were, and write up their notebooks accordingly. What usually happens is that one officer having written up his notebook, the other officer copies down the same thing. So you get two notebooks. Superintendent Hannam thought they could do just as well with one notebook and I, for my part, see nothing wrong in that.

'There is one thing in this case which seems to me to show that the police officers were maintaining to the highest degree the traditions of fairness that we hope govern the conduct of the police: that phrase "Murder? Can you prove it?" It could have been twisted to sound very nasty, could it not? Without altering the words the impression could have been given that what the Doctor was saying in effect was: "Well, murder; you know and I know and we all know that I did it, but you could never prove it." It could have been given that impression. You heard the evidence that Superintendent Hannam and Inspector Pugh both volunteered – it was not extracted in cross-examination – which gives it a wholly different meaning which is very much in favour of the defence, a meaning on which Mr Lawrence rightly relies, and which shows that this man, who must have known at this stage that something was going to happen, acted in such a way as to give the impression to experienced police officers that murder was the last thing he thought he was ever going to be charged with.'

'Second, what help, if any, can you get from the whole period of this illness *before* the 31st of October or the 1st of November, when, as it has been put, the design for murder begins? You have heard the Doctor's treatment criticized, and you have heard it defended; but how does it help you to answer the real question which in this case you have to answer? As stated by the prosecution – and indeed you may think to some extent on the admitted facts – it is not a very pretty story. Of course I can well understand a legacy being left to a doctor who is an old family friend or something of the sort, and the last thing I should wish to do would be to try to lay down terms and conditions under which doctors can properly receive legacies. But if you find a patient who is given drugs by a doctor, and a doctor angling for a legacy and expressing excessive anxiety for what he is likely to get under the will, when the doctor goes on holiday and is taken out of the will, and shortly before the patient's death is back in the will again, and then signs a form about cremation – well, there are many members of the medical profession who would tell the executor they could not have anything to do with such a legacy. . . . But there is a very very big difference between something of that sort and a charge of murder.

'Suppose you are going to come to the conclusion, as the prosecution invites you, that the Doctor was engaged in a sinister scheme. How does it help? In one way it weakens the case for the prosecution. Their case would be stronger if it could be said: there was a doctor who for two years had been treating a patient in a completely model way, doing the right thing at the right time, and then suddenly goes completely off the rails. In that sense, it is much weaker if the prosecution say they find a doctor giving wrong treatment right from the beginning at a time when they do not suggest he had murder in his mind. . . .' [Very urbane] 'Members of the jury, you may well come to the conclusion that the Doctor was a fraudulent rogue – indeed rogue would be too mild a word – who deliberately tried to get a patient under his influence to get something out of the patient; but all fraudulent rogues are not murderers. Fraud and murder are poles apart. . . . If you think, as you might think, that the truth about the treatment is somewhere between the two, that the Doctor administered drugs not with any sinister purpose in his mind but simply because he found it the easiest way to cope with a very difficult patient – if you thought that, does it help you when you come to the term murder? The prosecution must point to a specific date when they say the design was formed.' [Touch of factual dryness] 'You have to consider what was done in relation to the condition in which the patient was *then*, and not mind, it seems to me, one way or the other, how she got there.

'The third matter is – and I leap now to the very end – the doses of paraldehyde. You will remember there was great discussion at one time as to whether Nurse Randall really did give a second injection which is not recorded in the books. Does it help? The fact is, is it not, that on the case for the prosecution the Doctor had made up his mind to murder with the use of morphia and heroin. If that is so, you don't really need to bother about these two injections of paraldehyde. All they could have done at most was to accelerate the death by a few hours. And if the Doctor was not using morphia and heroin to bring about her death, then no one in their senses can suggest that one, or two, injections of paraldehyde at the very end themselves constitute murder. . . . '

And so this hardy point is at last at rest.

'Now I come to what is the last of what I call the inessentials – and that is the big discrepancy between the amounts of the drugs that were prescribed and the amounts that were administered and which are recorded in the books. . . . The prescriptions, of course, are no direct evidence of what was administered. Some link must be shown between the two; and the Attorney-General has submitted: Why do doctors prescribe drugs unless they intend them to be administered? Well, of course, they do not, and that raises a presumption, no doubt. But that presumption, as it seems to me, is completely rebutted if you get nurses coming and saying: "We have recorded the injections in writing, and these books contain all the injections that were given." It rebuts the presumption and makes it mere conjecture (upon which you can never act in a criminal case of any sort) that any drugs in excess of that were given. There is no direct evidence that the Doctor actually collected or received any of these drugs that are set down in the prescription list. . . . As to the special injections recorded in the books, some of them you will probably think are proved to your satisfaction as relating quite clearly to vitamins and so on. Others the prosecution point to, saying that they must have been morphia and heroin. That is a matter for you. But what seems to me quite clear is that the special injections cannot possibly account for the difference between the amounts prescribed and the amounts that were actually administered.'

Only four special injections were given between the 9th and the 12th of November, whereas the amount of morphia unaccounted for during that period was over 30 grains, and the heroin nearly 22 grains.

'. . . So you may think that those four special injections are quite incapable of accounting for the discrepancy.

'It is of course possible to say that the Doctor at any time when he was visiting Mrs Morell, and being alone in the room, gave her a large injection. No one can say that is inconceivable. It is possible that he told the nurse that he had given half a grain of morphia or half a grain of heroin, when he had given a much greater dose, but it is not that sort of conjecture upon which you can act when there is a charge of murder. You have got the medical history in the nurses' notes. If there had been anything in those notes which pointed to a much larger injection than that which is recorded, the doctors would have called your attention to it, but they have not. They are the skilled readers of these notes, not you and I. If the doctors could point to any injection about which they can say, "Well, we cannot understand how she had symptoms of that sort if the dose is as small as is recorded here," then you might have a genuine case which you could begin to investigate. But short of that, members of the jury, you have nothing except mere conjecture.

'Moreover, it is no use saying, "Oh, well, if *all* the difference was not given, then at least *something* more than was recorded must have been given." It is no use saying that, for this reason: that if that is the position, then there must be some channel existing by which the drugs prescribed were improperly disappearing; and once you accept the existence of such a channel, you could not be satisfied, could you, as to what the quantity was which was disappearing. In other words, if there was a channel, then there is nothing to show you that it did not account for the whole of the discrepancy.

'Was there in fact such a channel? Members of the jury, I come to a difficult part of the case, but a part you may want to face, and that I must help you to face so far as I can. Let me put it this way. Supposing you were to think – there are no grounds on which you can safely think so – but supposing you were to think that the Doctor had been dishonest about drugs, how much better would it be that you should unjustly suspect him of that sort of thing than that you should unjustly convict him of murder? . . . There must have been, must there not, carelessness or dishonesty somewhere. You may say, if you like, that there must have been some carelessness on the Doctor's part, that he ought to have noticed when these prescriptions were being made that he was prescribing for quantities that were far larger than the quantities which the nurses' books show to have been given. You might think that you ought to go further, and that in some way these drugs were disappearing in a way in which they ought not to. One knows that dangerous drugs are things in which there is an illicit traffic, and you might think that someone was dealing dishonestly with them, and that someone must either have been the Doctor himself or one of the nurses. If you were ever to get so far as to begin to wonder which of those people was most likely, you would in fairness to the Doctor have to bear in mind that two of the nurses have told lies about this matter in the witness-box. One of them lied about whether the drugs were kept locked or not – that was Nurse Stronach – one of the others, either Nurse Mason-Ellis or Nurse Randall, lied about the conversation in the train in which Nurse Randall is supposed to have said, "Don't you say that or you will get me into trouble"; either she said that or she did not, they could not both have been telling the truth about the matter.

'I hope most sincerely that no one will think that I am making accusations against anybody. . . . What I am inviting you to do is to disregard the whole matter as mere speculation. . . . As to the rest, the only safe thing to do when you have a charge of murder by the injection of drugs is to have regard only to those injections which have been clearly proved before you. . . . '

One of the beauties of a jury's verdict is its inassailableness. There are no explanations and no apologies. Once a foreman has spoken the one or the two words, that is the end of it. No juror, then or after, can be questioned on his verdict; what is more, no bench would listen to his second thoughts.

The day is nearly over when the Judge begins,

'Now, members of the jury, I come to what are the essentials in the case. There are three things that have to be proved, and the prosecution has to prove every one of them. It has to prove an act or acts of murder. It has to prove that those acts caused the death of Mrs Morell. It has to prove that at the time when those acts were committed by the Doctor, the Doctor intended to kill. Those are the three essentials.

'Let me begin with the second; whether the act caused death, because, as Mr Lawrence rightly submitted to you, if it did not, that finishes the whole of this inquiry. . . . He submitted that the immediate physical cause of death was not drugs at all. It was some intervening cause, such as another cerebral thrombosis, or just old age, just people dying (as Dr Harman put it). . . . Well, upon this, as upon so many other points in this case, you depend entirely, do you not, on the medical evidence. Dr Douthwaite's evidence was quite clear and uncompromising – he regarded the overdose of drugs as causing the death. Dr Ashby also, I think it is fair to say from his evidence, regarded that as being the most likely of the causes, but he could not exclude the other possibility beyond any shadow of doubt. Dr Ashby, coming between the extremes of Dr Douthwaite and Dr Harman, is rather the key witness in the case. Even if you think that what he was admitting was only a bare possibility, something that can never be quite ruled out, you have to put that concession of Dr Ashby's side by side with the evidence that you have got from Dr Harman. What Dr Harman said in effect was, "When you get an old lady of over eighty, and one who is suffering from cerebral thrombosis, she may die of anything at any time, and no one can say beyond reasonable doubt what it was that she actually died of."

'Members of the jury, I cannot give you more help than that....

It is for you to say whether you are satisfied that this lady did not in the end die by natural causes; and if you are not satisfied about that, the case for the prosecution ends there.'

'Now we come to what is perhaps the central part, the most essential of the three essential things – the act or acts of murder. It is a most curious situation, perhaps unique in these courts, that the act of murder has to be proved by expert evidence. Normally it is something that any jury can understand. Here it is the prosecution saying that the act is recorded somewhere in these books, but without a doctor to interpret the books they cannot begin to put their finger on what is suggested to be the act of murder. . . . It may be that the prosecution are in a much more difficult position in this case than they are in other cases. It may be that it is very much more difficult for the Crown ever to prove that a doctor murders his patient than it is to prove other acts of murder. It may be so, but that does not, in law, relieve them of the burden of proof that is upon them. . . . The prosecution identify three acts which they submit to you, and about which you must be satisfied that they amount to an act of murder. If you find some break in the policy, some change, something that the medical evidence says is clearly wrong and apparently inexplicable, that is enough for this stage, because you may then say, "There is an act that needs explanation". I am not bothering, at the moment, you see, about the intent; that comes at a later stage of the inquiry; at the moment we are simply looking, you and I, for some act that is capable of being described as a murderous act.

'The first is the dropping of the morphia with the intent that it should be reintroduced with fatal effect, which is the theory of Dr Douthwaite. Well, members of the jury, you heard Mr Lawrence on Friday inviting you in effect to ask yourselves whether you could have sufficient confidence to convict on a charge of murder upon a theory which the doctor himself did not think of until his examination in the witness-box was virtually completed. I do not think I need say more about it than this – that if you find a theory which the other doctor for the prosecution is not prepared to support and which the doctor for the defence says is wholly wrong – if indeed Dr Ashby did not equally say it was wrong – you might think that it would be far too dangerous to adopt the theory of Dr Douthwaite, whatever his qualifications may be and however impressed you may have been by the way in which he gave his evidence. . . .

'If you are of that view, then pass to the alternative acts. The prosecution say that you will find at or about November 8th a sudden change in the treatment for which there is no justifiable medical reason, and if you do find that sudden change then you may fairly say that it gives you an act which is capable of being a murderous act. Can you find it?

'Well, here again Dr Douthwaite's evidence is – I think – quite positive and uncompromising. . . . He was not willing to credit the Doctor even with ignorance or error. He could find no medical explanation other than that he certainly intended to cause death. Well, that is clear enough. It is Dr Ashby's evidence which you have to consider with the utmost care. . . . So I might perhaps just say this: the position of a doctor who gives evidence for the prosecution is obviously one of considerable difficulty. He can be completely positive, and that, of course, is what the lawyers – if I may so put it – like; they want precise evidence. But men of science cannot always give precise, clear, unqualified answers, particularly if they are dealing with an illness which occurred years ago at which they were not present and about which they have not even the clinical reports. . . . You may think that at times what Dr Ashby gave with one hand he took away with the other. That he was manifestly anxious to be fair, manifestly anxious not to go any further than he felt was justified, you can hardly doubt. He wanted to give both sides of the picture. . . . I cannot read through the whole of Dr Ashby's evidence; I doubt if it would help you if I did. You must remember that, as I have said, you are not sitting here as medical men, you are not sitting here even as a body of men who can call for these transcripts, read them over every day down to the sixteenth, and then compare one paragraph with another and endeavour to arrive at a conclusion. That is not the way in which in this country we convict of murder. We convict only if the witness can clearly supply from the witness-box the evidence to the jury who, as I say, have not got the transcript in front of them. If therefore you come to the conclusion that Dr Ashby's evidence on this vital point was border-line evidence, and if it does not leave you with the clear impression that this change, which you will remember he described as coming from the "keeping under", was something which was out of the ordinary course of treatment and accelerated death, well then, you must leave it. Unless you go the whole way with Dr Douthwaite on this point, you must say that Dr Ashby's evidence was border-line.' [Still without the slightest truck with oratory] 'And in the matter of murder you cannot act upon border-line evidence, and therefore you would not be safe in convicting. That must be your attitude in the end.'

And the court adjourns at the usual hour.

DAY SEVENTEEN

THE same crowded court; the same held silence; but stretched today, nervous, tense.

'You will remember, members of the jury, that we had reached what was the central and at the same time perhaps the most difficult part of the case, and that was the act of murder, whether there was something that stood out from the medical history or not. There are two interpretations of the medical history: one, that it was the natural result, the spiral taking its course, the Doctor coping with a situation which, however it had arisen, was in fact there; and the other that drugs were given in such quantities as, it was said, would show that a doctor of the Doctor's qualifications quite clearly meant death. Dr Ashby said in his examination-in-chief: " . . . I can see no justification for the doses given after November 8th. Perhaps 'no justification' is too strong. . . . The right course, I think, would have been to carry on with what may have been the necessary doses of the previous week to keep the patient in an hypnotic state. . . . " And in answer to me he said this: "The instruction to keep her under would be almost certain to accelerate death." Then I asked him: "And that is a conclusion a man of the Doctor's qualifications would have reached?", and he said: "Yes, I think an anaesthetist is particularly conversant with the dangers of a patient being unconscious or semi-conscious."

'In cross-examination Dr Ashby gave an answer on which Mr Lawrence strongly relies. Mr Lawrence had been putting to him his alternative interpretation, and he said at the end of it: "It may well be that the drugs after November 8th were given with the sole object of promoting her comfort?" Answer: "I think that is a possible interpretation."

'And later on Mr Lawrence was putting the same thing to him in relation to the spiral. "And the Doctor may well have come to the conclusion that there was no more point in a change, in an attempt to wean her, and that he must go on, that death would overtake the spiral?" Answer: "I would accept that." Question: "And then the case goes on and the Doctor is forced into the spiral until he reaches a point of no return?" Answer: "Yes." Question: "And then it is his major preoccupation to promote her comfort and ease distress?" Answer: "Yes." Question: "That is the impasse in which you said yesterday the Doctor and his patient were?" Answer: "Yes." Question: "Dr Ashby, all that I have been putting to you is a possible view of the case, is it not?" Answer: "Yes, I think it is."

'Well, members of the jury, Dr Ashby then accepts that as a possibility, although, of course, he holds to his own view as being the more probable of the two. Well, you can if you like, put that view together with the certainty – I do not think that is too high a word – almost certainty, at any rate, of Dr Douthwaite, and say the prosecution case is proved. But you must also consider whether you ought not to put Dr Ashby's view together with the evidence of Dr Harman. And Dr Harman is the reverse way round, as it were. *He* accepts Dr Ashby's view as a possibility, but he himself holds another view. At the very end of his evidence I asked him specifically how far he agreed with Dr Ashby about the drugs accelerating death. I asked: "Would you agree or not that the instructions to 'keep under' would accelerate death?" And Dr Harman answered: "No, I do not think that." Question: "Do you attach any significance to these instructions at all?" Answer: "They signify to me that the patient has got now to the stage of delirium in which she would have remained distressed, excited, and uncontrollable if she had not been under some influence of drugs. . . . " Question: "Therefore, in your view, they were the right and natural instructions to give?" Answer: "I would go further and say that sort of policy, if it was a policy, is quite common in such cases."

'Then I put to him Dr Ashby's answer: "The instruction to keep her under would be almost certain to accelerate death", and I said to him: "With that you disagree?", and he said: "I would put the emphasis the other way round, I would agree that it might have done so; but I should say that it would more probably have not."

'Well, there you have, members of the jury, the evidence on what is the essential part of the case, perhaps *the* crucial part. It was the part upon which Mr Lawrence made a very strong submission to me. The fact that I held that it was a matter for you to determine and not for me, does not mean he was not in a position to make a strong submission. On the evidence of Dr Ashby, he clearly was; and he has now been able to fortify it by the evidence of Dr Harman. *Each* link in the prosecution's chain must be strong enough to stand the strain. It does not matter how strong the other links are. . . .'

'If, however, you proceed further, if you decide in favour of the prosecution on those points, if you decide that Mrs Morell was killed by a piece of medically unjustifiable treatment given to her by the Doctor, you will then have to deal with the question of intent, whether it was done with the intention to murder.' Intention is something that exists in a man's mind. Apart from his own evidence, intention can only be proved by inferences that are drawn from his own acts, but his own evidence is most welcome. A man, after all, knows what is in his own mind. 'And if he goes into the witness-box and tells you, and you think he is telling the truth, you would have the best evidence available. It is fair to say that when you approach this last part of the case you necessarily lack that. . . .

'In considering this matter, then, of what was in the Doctor's mind, you must look at all the circumstances of the case. . . . Here we are on much easier ground. . . . We are out of the field of conflict which so far has been dominated by the experts, and are dealing with things which you and I can understand and weigh. . . . First, motive. The Crown is never bound to prove motive. But it is one of the things one looks for in connexion with intent. I take it from the Attorney-General's opening that the motive was the motive of gain – that he wished to acquire a legacy by the death of Mrs Morell.' Mr Lawrence submitted that the chest of silver was a very paltry reward for murder. 'And you may think it is. But there must be said in fairness to the other side that the Doctor displayed a considerable interest in acquiring some legacy under the will. But even so you may think that it was a paltry reward to stimulate a doctor into committing murder, and, if the prosecution is right, laying long plans in advance. . . . Mr Lawrence's point does not rest there. He says that this is not a case of dealing out death in order to get a legacy from a strong and hearty woman. This was a woman who, admittedly, was dying. On the first of November she had from a few weeks to two months to live. If the Doctor had calculated that, he would have said to himself, would he not, "Well, she may be dead in two or three weeks and then I will get the chest I have been waiting for so long." Is he likely, it may be asked, to adopt a plan which does not even mean an instantaneous dose which kills her off, but involves a rather elaborate system of change in medication which takes thirteen days to dispose of her? If one takes the lowest estimate it would have meant that he would have had his chest of silver seven days before he would otherwise have had it. (There was at one time, I thought, a suggestion made that she would alter her will, but I do not think that has been pursued. And it is difficult to think that she was in any condition in this last time in November to have effectively altered her will.) Well, that is the point that Mr Lawrence put before you. He said that the suggestion that the Doctor had anticipated her death by a few days or weeks for the sake of a chest of silver worth £270 was ludicrous. Ludicrous is a strong word. But, members of the jury, it is a *strong* point. I listened carefully to the Attorney-General's speech to hear what the answer was. I did not hear the answer.'

The next circumstance to be considered is the false filling up of the cremation form. 'And I say false advisedly, for though it is a matter for you to decide, it seems to me that it was false.' Mr Lawrence stressed the importance of what was essential about this form – that it was not what the actual position *was*, whether or not the Doctor was legally entitled to anything, but whether *he thought* he was. 'Well, the answer which the Doctor gave to Superintendent Hannam – which is the only evidence we have – makes it plain that he knew, or thought he knew, he was going to get the chest of silver and the car. The Doctor did not say, "I thought I did not get it under the will, but by the gift or favour of the relatives." He did not give that as his explanation. He gave the explanation that he wanted to smooth the way for cremation. That explanation may or may not be satisfactory to you, but you have to remember that it is one thing to give it to a police officer and another thing to go into the witness-box and say it on oath and subject to cross-examination and testing.'

(This seems to leave room still for the possibility of the Doctor's having been genuinely mixed up when he was asked in 1956 about what he knew at the time of the cremation form. There had been so many technical changes that he might well have come to believe later on that he had always known the things were left to him.)

'The Attorney-General has laid stress on the statements the Doctor made to Superintendent Hannam, and some of them are difficult to justify on the evidence as we know it now: that she was in "terrible agony" at the end, for example. We know very clearly now that she was not. Perhaps that was a lapse of memory and quite understandable. But, again, you might have liked to have heard his own explanation about it. You might have liked to have heard, too, his own explanation about "easing the passing", a phrase which might be used quite innocently, but, on the other hand, a phrase which might perhaps go further. However, you must take into account not isolated phrases but the trend of his statements on the whole, and it seems to me that the statements as a whole do show from the beginning to the end that it had never crossed his mind that he was faced, or might be faced, with the charge of murdering Mrs Morell.

'... Take the chance interview last October. At the end of it the superintendent said to him, "I hope I shall finish all these inquiries soon, and we will probably have another talk"; and the Doctor answered, "Don't hurry; please be thorough; it is in my own interest. Good night, and thank you very much for your kindness." If he was the calculating murderer who felt that perhaps his sins were finding him out, one might have expected him to be very wary in the statements he was making; in fact he gave away a good deal at the particular interview when he said he knew about the Rolls-Royce and the silver....

'And when he was asked at the time of the search about drugs, there was that key sentence at the end, "I am not dishonest about drugs." It shows – does it not? – that what he thought he was being confronted with was some suggestion that he had been engaged in some sort of illicit traffic – prescribing more than he ought to have prescribed, or something of that sort – but not murder. And that last interview at the very end, of which I remind you, at which he was stunned and shocked by the idea of murder. . . .'

'I think there is only one other matter to which I need refer you in this part of the argument, and that is the point made by the Attorney-General on Friday about the nurses' notebooks. He asked: Where did they come from? Where had they been? In whose interest was it to keep them? I do not see a mystery here, but it is something one would have liked to know about. . . . Mr Lawrence has not anticipated the point and he did not deal with it in his final address to you; but if he had he might perhaps have asked a rhetorical question too. "What does the prosecution say these books prove – innocence or guilt? If guilt, why did the Doctor preserve them? If they prove innocence, then surely it does not matter where they come from or who has been keeping them?" '

This does perhaps not entirely meet the Attorney-General's point which was that if the Doctor had formed a design for murder he would have taken good care to arrange things so that the nursing entries would not look too bad for him.

And now a rallying of tone, a note of condensed firmness that indicates the end is near.

'Members of the jury, I can now sum up the whole issue for you, and I sum up for you just once again because it is important that you should not think that it is only the last point that I have been talking about that counts.

'There are three points, are there not? The Crown must satisfy you that Mrs Morell did not die from natural causes. If it fails to satisfy you of that, you acquit. If it satisfies you, you ask the next question. The Crown must satisfy you that there emerges an act of killing, something which is capable of being murderous. Again, if it fails to satisfy you of that, you acquit. If it succeeds – and only if it succeeds – you go on to the third question. The Crown must satisfy you that if there was an act of that sort, it was done with intent to murder. If it does not satisfy you of that, you acquit; and if it does satisfy you then you convict.

'Mr Lawrence has submitted to you that the whole case against the Doctor, from beginning to end, is merely suspicion. It may be so. . . . It may be that if this inquiry were ever to be completed the Doctor might appear as a man misjudged by those who suspected him – not a man wrongly prosecuted: no one, I think, can say that the Crown was not justified on the material they had at the beginning of this trial in prosecuting the Doctor – but a man who, if all the facts were known, was guilty of folly, perhaps worse than folly, but who never in his mind came within thought of murder. It may be so. . . . Who can say? Not you, members of the jury. Not you. It is not your task to say so. You have not heard the man who knows most about his own mind. . . . You do not sit as a court of inquiry to determine just how or why Mrs Morell died. You sit to answer one limited question: Has the prosecution satisfied you beyond reasonable doubt that the Doctor murdered Mrs Morell? On that question the Doctor stood on his rights and did not speak. I have made it quite clear that I am not criticizing that. I do not criticize it at all.' [With a measure of fervour] 'I hope that the day will never come when that right is denied to any Englishman. It is not a refuge of technicality: the law on this matter reflects the natural thought of England. So great is our horror at the idea that a man might be questioned, forced to speak and perhaps to condemn himself out of his own mouth,' [for the first time without detachment] 'that we afford to everyone suspected or accused of a crime, at every stage, and to the very end, the right to say: "Ask me no questions, I shall answer none. Prove your case."

'. . . And so this long process ends with the question with which it began: "Murder? Can you prove it?"

'I dare say it is the first time that you have sat in that jury-box. It is not the first time that I have sat in this chair. And not infrequently I have heard a case presented by the prosecution that seemed to me to be manifestly a strong one, and sometimes I have felt it my duty to tell the jury so. I do not think, therefore, that I ought to hesitate to tell you that here the case for the defence seems to me to be manifestly a strong one. . . . But it is the same question in the end, always the same – is the case for the Crown strong enough to carry conviction to your mind? It is your question. You have to answer it. It lies always with you, the jury. Always with you. And you will now consider what that answer shall be.'

*

The jury is led off immediately, the time is 11.16. The Doctor is made to disappear into his waiting cell below-stairs. Then the Judge leaves, too. Gradually the court empties, people drift out into the hall, stand about in groups, talking, smoking, pacing. . . .

'Will they be long?'
'You can't tell.'
'He made it pretty clear. . . .'
'I suppose so.'

'Not much doubt, is there?'
'Yeah.'
'You never can tell with them, though.'
'I guess not.'

'Judge practically *told* them.'
'So he didn't do it?'
'My dear chap, what a time to ask!'
'What if they can't agree? Then what?'
'Oh, you never can tell with them.'

'Don't they always put pressure on the twelfth man or something?'
'God knows what they do.'
'Well, when they want to go home?'
'Why can't they do it by majority like everybody else. . . .'
'*Unanimity.*'
'It doesn't seem human.'
'A criminal conviction is supposed to be based on the absence of reasonable doubt. If you had two or three of them dissent, it'd show there was doubt.'
'Oh, don't let's have *that* again. What I want to know is, will they be *long*?'

'. . . All he said was it wasn't safe to be sure.'
'He told them it wasn't a very strong case.'
'He told them they might find it wasn't *proved.*'
'There is no such thing in English law. The man's got to be one thing or the other.'

'I shouldn't like to be in his shoes – either way.'

'It doesn't seem very satisfactory.'

'It's the best we can do.'

'No. *Not* in his shoes.'

For what the Doctor is undergoing now, for what he has undergone in the last days, weeks, months, for what he will undergo, for what will mark him, in the years to come, is there (assuming him to be innocent, assuming him about to be acquitted) reparation? Is there comfort, consolation, return? Is there rhyme and reason? Reparation, on the immediate and material level, no. A man accused of murder, with whatever aloofness the law may have held him innocent before the verdict, is nearly always presumed not to have been quite that after his acquittal. In the Doctor's case the world, to a spectacular and rare degree – nature finely spurred by newspapers – did not even presume him innocent before his trial. Doubt, reasonable and unreasonable, will hang about him to the end of his days and after. His life will be broken, or, if one chooses to put it in another way, changed. Nor is he likely to get official redress – has not a case strong enough to go to a jury been made out – in terms of wrongful prosecution or imprisonment; he will not even get a soothing form of words. Comforts, then, compensations? Perhaps. By some fortunate workings of the law of diminishing returns, our capacities for suffering are not infinitely extendable. We bear; and may derive strength from having borne, comfort from being still there, comfort from any mercy: the faith of friends, the match struck by a stranger, discovery of reserves. (During the trial, while almost everyone in street or drawing-room was animated by the casual conviction of course, he must have done it – a conviction by no means shared by all who were in court – everyone who knew him, his friends and patients, is said to have been matter-of-factly certain of the Doctor's innocence.) There is compensation – always! and short-lived – in sheer relief: it is over; I may go now; the first steps, the taste of air. Yes; but these are mitigations, themselves contingent on disaster, the mountain's mice. . . . Why did disaster fall? On this man and not another? Can we ever answer, can we ever cease to ask that question? The usual conjunction, then, ill-starred, of circumstance and character? 'A man guilty of folly; but folly and murder are poles apart.' So are, for most of us, folly and the extremes of retribution, folly and utter downfall. Why on this fool and not on that? Why not on me? There but for the grace of God. . . . But why did the grace of God choose thus? Life, one might say, has a way of throwing up strange twists – who can tell? – without this piece of bad luck, without that loss, that outright catastrophe, I might never have seen, have met, have known; I would not have had that chance; I should not now be *here*. . . . It was all for the best. Do we really say that, and how often? Ought we to say it for another? '*Nous avons tous assez de force pour supporter les maux d'autrui.*' Always fortitude enough, words enough, to explain away another man's misfortune. . . . Can we let it go at that, can we turn now from the Doctor's fate with the sense that, somehow, in some way, all is well; or must we accept that his entanglement was another tale told by an idiot?

'They're coming back – '

There is a stampede into court. Through the door at the far end the jury file in one by one – do they step lightly? – settle themselves, consciously, in the box. It is noon: they have been out forty-four minutes. The foreman has not sat down. The Doctor is signed to get up, too. In the dock, the warder is suddenly at his elbow. Everything is seen to be happening as if it were standing still, with time palpably hanging between each motion. 'And have you reached your verdict?', the foreman's non-carrying voice saying, Yes; another cumulus of time and the foreman's non-carrying voice, Not Guilty, the Doctor buckling as if to sit down and prodded up again, the moment smoothly bridged by the Judge, 'Mr Attorney, there is another indictment – ' the much rumoured, the denied, the half-believed' now fact; the Attorney-General's voice fading up, ' . . . the further indictment charging the Doctor with the murder of Mrs Hullett – ' the impression, uncertain, shocked, that he is now so charged; the Attorney-General more audible, ' . . . even more difficult to secure a fair trial . . . this indictment based on, unsupported, evidence of an administration of drugs . . . the ordeal of a further trial on a charge of murder . . . a *nolle prosequi* – ' the Doctor standing, unmoving, limp, letting it wash past; the Judge's,

'... all further proceedings on the indictment are stayed in this court –' the Judge raising his face to the dock; the clear, cool, colourless voice: the Doctor's full name, 'you are now discharged –' the Doctor just framing the words, toneless, Thank you; making his small grave bow, keeping his eyes, intent, unblinking, on the Judge; the Judge staring back at him, blank and earnest; the Doctor, half stumbling, half helped, vanishing from sight; Mr Lawrence rising to ask for bail on some offences under the Drugs Act come to light in the course of this microscopic investigation; bail fusslessly granted; the Judge thanking the jury with ceremony and near emotion, 'your labours have been exceptional. ... I therefore discharge each of you from jury service for the rest of your lives ...'; the Judge's swift exit, the pattern broken, the slow dispersal. ...

Outside, the siege of the first day is on. The streets are solid with people and police. News photographers tear from door to likely back-door. Dogged, unmovable, hours after, the massed hundreds wait. They will not see him. The Doctor has been helped out of the building and borne to a place of safe concealment by the potent offices of a friendly newspaper.

A CHOICE OF PENGUINS

A Better Class of Person John Osborne

The playwright's autobiography, 1929–56. 'Splendidly enjoyable' – John Mortimer. 'One of the best, richest and most bitterly truthful autobiographies that I have ever read' – Melvyn Bragg

Out of Africa Karen Blixen (Isak Dinesen)

After the failure of her coffee-farm in Kenya, where she lived from 1913 to 1931, Karen Blixen went home to Denmark and wrote this unforgettable account of her experiences. 'No reader can put the book down without some share in the author's poignant farewell to her farm' – *Observer*

In My Wildest Dreams Leslie Thomas

The autobiography of Leslie Thomas, author of *The Magic Army* and *The Dearest and the Best*. From Barnardo boy to original virgin soldier, from apprentice journalist to famous novelist, it is an amazing story. 'Hugely enjoyable' – *Daily Express*

The Winning Streak Walter Goldsmith and David Clutterbuck

Marks and Spencer, Saatchi and Saatchi, United Biscuits, G.E.C. . . The U.K.'s top companies reveal their formulas for success, in an important and stimulating book that no British manager can afford to ignore.

Mind Tools Rudy Rucker

Information is the master concept of the computer age, which throws a completely new light on the age-old concepts of space and number, logic and infinity. In *Mind Tools* Rudy Rucker has produced the most charming and challenging intellectual carnival since *Gödel, Escher, Bach*.

Bird of Life, Bird of Death Jonathan Evan Maslow

In the summer of 1983 Jonathan Maslow set out to find the quetzal. In doing so, he placed himself between the natural and unnatural histories of Central America, between the vulnerable magnificence of nature and the terrible destructiveness of man. 'A wonderful book' – *The New York Times Book Review*

A CHOICE OF PENGUINS

Adieux: A Farewell to Sartre Simone de Beauvoir

A devastatingly frank account of the last years of Sartre's life, and his death, by the woman who for more than half a century shared that life. 'A true labour of love, there is about it a touching sadness, a mingling of the personal with the impersonal and timeless which Sartre himself would surely have liked and understood' – *Listener*

Business Wargames James Barrie

How did BMW overtake Mercedes? Why did Laker crash? How did MacDonalds grab the hamburger market? Drawing on the tragic mistakes and brilliant victories of military history, this remarkable book draws countless fascinating parallels with case histories from industry worldwide.

Metamagical Themas Douglas R. Hofstadter

This astonishing sequel to the bestselling, Pulitzer Prize-winning *Gödel, Escher, Bach* swarms with 'extraordinary ideas, brilliant fables, deep philosophical questions and Carrollian word play' – Martin Gardner

Into the Heart of Borneo Redmond O'Hanlon

'Perceptive, hilarious and at the same time a serious natural-history journey into one of the last remaining unspoilt paradises' – *New Statesman* 'Consistently exciting, often funny and erudite without ever being overwhelming' – *Punch*

The Assassination of Federico García Lorca Ian Gibson

Lorca's 'crime' was his antipathy to pomposity, conformity and intolerance. His punishment was murder. Ian Gibson reveals the truth about Lorca's death and the atmosphere in Spain that allowed it to happen.

The Secrets of a Woman's Heart Hilary Spurling

The later life of Ivy Compton-Burnett 1920–69. 'A biographical triumph . . . elegant, stylish, witty tender, immensely acute – dazzles and exhilarates . . . a great achievement' – Kay Dick in the *Literary Review*. 'One of the most important literary biographies of the century' – *New Statesman*

A CHOICE OF PENGUINS

Beyond the Blue Horizon Alexander Frater

The romance and excitement of the legendary Imperial Airways Eastbound Empire service – the world's longest and most adventurous scheduled air route – relived fifty years later in one of the most original travel books of the decade. 'The find of the year' – *Today*

Voyage through the Antarctic Richard Adams and Ronald Lockley

Here is the true, authentic Antarctic of today, brought vividly to life by Richard Adams, author of *Watership Down*, and Ronald Lockley, the world-famous naturalist. 'A good adventure story, with a lot of information and a deal of enthusiasm for Antarctica and its animals' – *Nature*

Getting to Know the General Graham Greene

'In August 1981 my bag was packed for my fifth visit to Panama when the news came to me over the telephone of the death of General Omar Torrijos Herrera, my friend and host . . .' 'Vigorous, deeply felt, at times funny, and for Greene surprisingly frank' – *Sunday Times*

The Search for the Virus Steve Connor and Sharon Kingman

In this gripping book, two leading *New Scientist* journalists tell the remarkable story of how researchers discovered the AIDS virus and examine the links between AIDS and lifestyles. They also look at the progress being made in isolating the virus and finding a cure.

Arabian Sands Wilfred Thesiger

'In the tradition of Burton, Doughty, Lawrence, Philby and Thomas, it is, very likely, the book about Arabia to end all books about Arabia' – *Daily Telegraph*

When the Wind Blows Raymond Briggs

'A visual parable against nuclear war: all the more chilling for being in the form of a strip cartoon' – *Sunday Times* 'The most eloquent anti-Bomb statement you are likely to read' – *Daily Mail*

A CHOICE OF PENGUINS

The Diary of Virginia Woolf
Five volumes edited by Quentin Bell and Anne Olivier Bell

'As an account of intellectual and cultural life of our century, Virginia Woolf's diaries are invaluable; as the record of one bruised and unquiet mind, they are unique' – Peter Ackroyd in the *Sunday Times*

Voices of the Old Sea Norman Lewis

'I will wager that *Voices of the Old Sea* will be a classic in the literature about Spain' – *Mail on Sunday* 'Limpidly and lovingly Norman Lewis has caught the helpless, unwitting, often foolish, but always hopeful village in its dying summers, and saved the tragedy with sublime comedy' – *Observer*

The First World War A J P Taylor

In this superb illustrated history, A J P Taylor 'manages to say almost everything that is important for an understanding and, indeed, intellectual digestion of that vast event . . . A special text . . . a remarkable collection of photographs' – *Observer*

Ninety-Two Days Evelyn Waugh

With characteristic honesty Evelyn Waugh here debunks the romantic notions attached to rough travelling; his journey in Guiana and Brazil is difficult, dangerous and extremely uncomfortable, and his account of it is witty and unquestionably compelling.

When the Mind Hears Harlan Lane
A History of the Deaf

'Reads like a suspense novel . . . what emerges is evidence of a great wrong done to a minority group, the deaf' – *The New York Times Book Review* 'Impassioned, polemical, at times even virulent . . . (he shows) immense scholarship, powers of historical reconstruction, and deep empathy for the world of the deaf' – Oliver Sacks in *The New York Review of Books*

A CHOICE OF PENGUINS

Trail of Havoc Patrick Marnham

In this brilliant piece of detective work, Patrick Marnham has traced the steps of Lord Lucan from the fateful night of 7th November 1974 when he murdered his children's nanny and attempted to kill his ex-wife. As well as being a fascinating investigation, the book is also a brilliant portrayal of a privileged section of society living under great stress.

Light Years Gary Kinder

Eduard Meier, an uneducated Swiss farmer, claims since 1975 to have had over 100 UFO sightings and encounters with 'beamships' from the Pleiades. His evidence is such that even the most die-hard sceptics have been unable to explain away the phenomenon.

And the Band Played On Randy Shilts
Politics, people and the AIDS epidemic

Written after years of extensive research by the only American journalist to cover the epidemic full-time, the book is a masterpiece of reportage and a tragic record of mismanaged institutions and scientific vendettas, of sexual politics and personal suffering.

The Return of a Native Reporter Robert Chesshyre

Robert Chesshyre returned to Britain from the United States in 1985 where he had spent four years as the *Observer*'s correspondent. This is his devastating account of the country he came home to: intolerant, brutal, grasping and politically and economically divided. It is a nation, he asserts, struggling to find a role.

Women and Love Shere Hite

In this culmination of *The Hite Report* trilogy, 4,500 women provide an eloquent testimony of the disturbingly unsatisfying nature of their emotional relationships and point to what they see as the causes. *Women and Love* reveals a new cultural perspective in formation: as women change the emotional structure of their lives, they are defining a fundamental debate over the future of our society.

PENGUIN TRUE CRIME

A series of brilliant investigations into some of the most mysterious and baffling crimes ever committed. *Titles published and forthcoming:*

Crippen: The Mild Murderer Tom Cullen
The famous story of the doctor who poisoned his wife and buried her in the cellar.

Who Killed Hanratty? Paul Foot
An investigation into the notorious A6 murder.

Norman Birkett H. Montgomery Hyde
The biography of one of Britain's most humane and respected judges.

The Complete Jack the Ripper Donald Rumbelow
An investigation into the identity of the most elusive murderer of all time.

The Riddle of Birdhurst Rise R. Whittington-Egan
The Croydon Poisoning Mystery of 1928–9.

Suddenly at the Priory John Williams
Who poisoned the Victorian barrister Charles Bravo?

Stinie: Murder on the Common Andrew Rose
The truth behind the Clapham Common murder.

The Poisoned Life of Mrs Maybrick Bernard Ryan
Mr Maybrick died of arsenic poisoning – how?

The Gatton Mystery J. and D. Gibney
The great unsolved Australian triple murder.

Earth to Earth John Cornwell
Who killed the Luxtons in their remote mid-Devon farmhouse?

The Ordeal of Philip Yale Drew R. Whittington-Egan
A real life murder melodrama in three acts.

Famous Trials of Marshall Hall Edward Marjoribanks
The authoritative life of the most distinguished advocate of his generation.